A Black Woman's Odyssey
Through Russia and Jamaica:
The Narrative of Nancy Prince

A Black Woman's Odyssey Through Russia and Jamaica:

The Narrative of Nancy Prince

Introduction
by
Ronald G. Walters

M.W. Markus Wiener Publishing
New York

First edition published by Markus Wiener Publishing, 1990

© Copyright, 1990 for the introduction by Ronald G. Walters

Library of Congress Cataloging-in-Publication Data

Prince, Nancy, b. 1799.
  [Narrative of the life and travels of Mrs. Nancy Prince]
  A Black woman's odyssey through Russia and Jamaica : the narrative of Nancy Prince / introduction by Ronald G. Walters.
      p.   cm. — (Topics in world history)
  Reprint, with new introd. Originally published: A narrative of the life and travels of Mrs. Nancy Prince, Boston : N. Prince, 1850.
  Includes bibliographical references
  ISBN 1-55876-019-9
    1. Prince, Nancy, b. 1799—Journeys.   2. Afro-Americans—Biography.   3. Soviet Union—Description and travel.   4. Soviet Union—Social life and customs—1533–1917.   5. Jamaica—Description and travel.   I. Title.   II. Series.
  E185.97.P94A3   1989
  973'.049607302—do20
  [B]   89-24945
                                                            CIP

Cover Design by Cheryl Mirkin

Printed in The United States of America

To Rose Walters,
another intrepid woman.

Introduction

by

Ronald G. Walters
Johns Hopkins University

Nancy Gardner Prince's *Narrative* is an adventure story, an enigma, and a treasure. First published in 1850, her book stands as one of the few surviving autobiographical accounts by a free black woman in the pre-Civil War North.[1] The handful of comparable narratives may reveal more of the inner lives of their authors, but none can match hers for exotic settings and remarkable happenings. Mrs. Prince, as she called herself, was frequently present when great and exciting events occurred. She was in Russia during the terrible St. Petersburg flood of 1824, as well as during the succession crisis and Decembrist Revolt of the following year. She travelled to live and work in Jamaica during a period of turmoil following the end of slavery on the island. A gritty and determined woman, she survived natural disasters, near-capture by pirates, and a shipwreck. She rescued her sister from a brothel, and participated in the antislavery and women's rights movements of her day. Exciting as it is, however, her story is almost as intriguing for what lies between the lines as for what appears on the printed page. At its heart is embedded the elusive spirit of Nancy Prince herself.

We know little about the author beyond what she tells us. Her family was among the roughly 6,500 free African-Americans living in Massachusetts at the time of her birth in 1799. Perhaps more than most of her contemporaries, white or black, she seems to have grown up moving among a variety of cultures. Some of her family were servants to well-known New Englanders—an experience that brought them into close contact with the manners and mores of prosperous, pious, and learned whites. At home, the *Narrative* makes clear, the children heard proud stories of Africa from both her grandfather and her mother's third husband; Mrs. Prince may even have absorbed some Indian lore by way of her grandmother. In addition, Prince's grandfather, stepfather, brother, and husband were sailors. This was a common occupation among free African-American men in New England; the sea offered opportunities they could not find on land, and they were represented among seamen far out of proportion to their percentage in the general population.[2] As she notes about her brother George's decision to take to the sea, the occupation promised "comfort and respectability" for families ashore. For

Nancy Prince, a maritime heritage meant that as a child and young woman she heard tales of faraway places, stirring adventures, and exotic ways of life. Her background prepared her well to be an observer and a fearless traveller.

Nancy Prince's childhood was disrupted—as many were in her day—by death and poverty. She never knew her father, who died shortly after her birth. That, and the removal of the family for whom he worked from Newburyport to Boston, was doubtless what sent her mother first to her father's home in Gloucester and then into her third marriage to a man who would later be taken off an American ship and impressed into naval service by a British privateer during the War of 1812. He died "oppressed, in the English dominions," leaving his young wife with eight children. Nancy Prince described her stepfather as a good provider, but not particularly kind to her or her sister by her mother's earlier marriage. Her life, however, took a turn for the worse when he died. His death marked for Prince the beginning of a period of instability and illness, during which she, like many other nineteenth-century children, moved from household to household, living with various combinations of relatives and strangers and working extremely hard. If childhood offered Nancy Prince few joys, she nevertheless found comfort as she became an adult. In Boston, shortly before her twentieth birthday, she had herself baptized—

the symbolic birth of the deep religious commitment that pervades her story. She "found peace with God" in a life otherwise lacking tranquility.

Nancy Prince's religious commitment, along with her race and gender, shaped her persistent involvement in reform activities. In common with other evangelical Protestant New Englanders, black and white, she was attracted to a variety of moral and religious crusades, both at home and abroad. Her decision to go to Jamaica in 1840 was made following a lecture, and a meeting with a missionary who had spent seven years on the island. Prior to that she had been drawn to Massachusetts' passionate brand of antislavery, a cause dominated by William Lloyd Garrison, who called for immediate emancipation and who was willing to accept no compromise with slaveholding. After 1837, feuds over political participation and the role of women in the movement left Mrs. Prince disillusioned with organized abolitionism, but her hatred of slavery remained unmitigated.

Most of Mrs. Prince's reform activities were typical of the antebellum period and quite respectable. In Massachusetts, Russia, and Jamaica she was active in attempts to establish schools, asylums, and programs of spiritual instruction, mostly for the benefit of children. Such projects were reasonably common among religious and genteel New England women.

Mrs. Prince, however, was far less conventional—and anything but genteel—in her attacks upon slavery and discrimination against women. Late in his life, one observer recalled a day in 1847 when Nancy Prince, whom he called "a colored woman of prominence," led a group of African-Americans in attacking a slave catcher attempting to capture a runaway from the South. She and her companions threw him out of a house and pelted him with stones until he fled. Seven years later, in spite of the infirmity and poverty that impelled her to write her *Narrative,* she appeared before a Woman's Rights Convention in Philadelphia and recounted some of the experiences described in her book. Typically, she "invoked the blessing of God" upon this radical enterprise, adding that "she understood woman's wrongs better than woman's rights. . . ."[3]

Spirited as Nancy Prince was, her story would never have been written if she had remained in Massachusetts, taken the few forms of work available to free black women, and participated in religious and reform activities. It was marriage to an older man, apparently to escape the unhappiness of her family life, that set her off on her adventures. Nero Prince, whose first name Nancy never mentions, was among a small number of blacks employed at the Russian court since the reign of Peter the Great (1682–1725), if not earlier.[4] His origins

are obscure; one highly romantic account
claims that he was a Russian Jew who some-
how came to America and "identified himself
with the colored people."[5] More plausible is
Mrs. Prince's matter-of-fact statement that he
was from Marlborough, Massachusetts. Whatever his background, Nero Prince was a man of
high standing in Boston's African-American
community. He was a founding member of the
first black Freemason's Lodge in America and
became its second Grand Master in 1807. It is
not clear how much older he was than his wife;
the same highly-flawed account that portrayed
him as a Russian Jew also had him dying in
1825 at age eightyseven, almost a decade before
his actual death. If these numbers had been
accurate, husband and wife would have been
born sixty-one years apart. The real age difference was probably smaller, but still considerable. Far more certain is that Nero Prince was
an impressive man in his own right, whose
dignity and seafaring connections earned him
his position at the Tsar's court, as well as the
hand of a much younger woman. "I made up
my mind to leave my country," Nancy Gardner
recalled. With Nero Prince, she accomplished
her end.

In Russia, Mrs. Prince was well-positioned
to exercise her talents as an observer. Writing at
a time when foreign travellers frequently
treated native customs with disdain, Mrs.
Prince was remarkably even-handed in de-

scribing Russian practices, even those that surely must have offended her Protestant and egalitarian sensibilities. Her multi-cultural upbringing, her status as an outsider in America, and her appreciation of the lack of racial prejudice she found in her new home may all have contributed to her tolerant portrayal of manners and beliefs that she could scarcely have imagined as a young woman in Massachusetts.

Everyday life, however, was not all that Mrs. Prince saw while in Russia. She happened to be in St. Petersburg at an extraordinary time. In 1824 a great flood struck the city and nearly cost Nancy Prince her life. It also led her to write a description in her *Narrative* that the authority on blacks in Russia finds "strikingly reminiscent" of Alexander Pushkin's more famous account.[6] Even greater historical events unfolded over the following two years.

In December, 1825, Tsar Alexander I died, setting off a series of crises. Alexander, whose childhood had been dominated by his grandmother, Catherine the Great, ascended to the throne upon the murder of his crazed father in 1801, as part of a conspiracy in which he may have been involved. Contemporaries and historians found his personality to be puzzling and intriguing. A major figure in the defeat of Napoleon and the restructuring of Europe in the years that followed, Alexander had lost an earlier commitment to reform by the time Mrs. Prince came to Russia, and had become

moody, isolated, and mystical. His death spar-
ked confusion and turmoil.

As an American in a land far different from
her own, Mrs. Prince may not have understood
all that was at issue in Russia in 1825–6. What
she did capture quite well, nonetheless, was
the uncertainty surrounding the succession to
the throne—it was not widely known that Alexander's brother Constantine had renounced
his claim in favor of a younger sibling, Nicholas. While the true succession remained in
doubt, a group of military officers and nobles
thought they saw an opportunity to seize
power; their uprising was known as the Decembrist Revolt. Although it was the fruit of
years of plotting for the abolition of serfdom
and the establishment of constitutional government, the attempt at toppling the regime
was ill-conceived and, as Mrs. Prince relates,
thoroughly crushed. Its futility notwithstanding, the insurrection was a dramatic and important moment in Russian history. Although
Mrs. Prince shed tears over the fate of the
rebels, she found Nicholas I and his wife to be
"courteous and affable," as the new Tsar could
be with his family and others around him.
History would be less kind to the man who put
down the Decembrist Revolt, thwarted political reform, and increased the repressive power
of the state police.

After nine and a half years' absence, Nancy
Prince returned to America in 1833 to regain

her health and to rebuild her life without her husband—who died in Russia before rejoining her—or her mother and sister. It was during this time that she began to engage in antislavery and other reform movements. She may also have helped support herself by speaking about her life abroad. In 1839 the antislavery newspaper, *Liberator,* carried a small notice announcing a lecture by her "on the manners and customs of Russia."[7] There was a restless energy to Nancy Prince, however, and it is not surprising that she would again feel called to leave her native land. This time Jamaica provided the inspiration.

In the same month that Mrs. Prince left Russia for the United States—August, 1833—another historical event took place that would shape her life: the British Parliament passed the Emancipation Act providing for the eventual freedom of all slaves in its New World colonies. The legislation was to take effect on August 1, 1834. All slave children under six years of age became free immediately; for the remaining slaves, the Act set up a system of apprenticeship under which field hands would have to labor until 1840. Domestic slaves would be freed two years earlier, in 1838. During this transitional period of apprenticeship, ex-slaves worked forty-five hours a week for their masters, with the remainder of their time belonging to them. The Act also provided compensation to masters for the loss of their slave property. The legislation was not the immediate and uncompensated emancipation American abolitionists like Mrs. Prince demanded, but Britain's commitment to end slavery filled them with hope—for years afterward some of their number celebrated August 1, rather than July 4, as the true birthday of freedom in the New World.

By August 1, 1838, two years before Mrs. Prince's arrival, the apprenticeship system had broken down in Jamaica, and the local Assembly begrudgingly granted full freedom to all blacks on the island. Missionaries from Britain and the United States seized the opportunity to reap a harvest of souls among the newly liberated Afro-Jamaicans—the number of Baptists, for example, shot up from 10,000 before the Emancipation Act to 34,000 in 1845.[8] For a time, Mrs. Prince was caught up in the enthusiasm. Eventually, however, her zeal for saving souls in Jamaica cooled after exposure to mercenary and deceitful missionaries who failed to rise to her spiritual and ethical standards.

In Russia, she had been more an observer than a participant, in spite of her charitable activities and her brush with death in the 1824 flood. Jamaica, however, set the stage for Nancy Prince's most perilous adventures—thanks to pirates, unseaworthy vessels, and deceitful captains—and provided her with a new field of action. Her mission was both religious and racial. As she put it, she "hoped that

I might aid, in some small degree, to raise up and encourage the emancipated inhabitants, and teach the young children to read and work, to fear God, and put their trust in the Savior." From the pen of a white woman, those words might sound patronizing, an expression of a missionary impulse to bring enlightenment to the supposedly unenlightened. Mrs. Prince's agenda, like that of other African-Americans who worked among the freedmen of the Caribbean and, later, in the southern United States, was more complex. To some extent she was, like her white counterparts, an agent of evangelical Protestantism and middle-class virtues who had little patience with other religions, or with what she regarded as immorality. Yet she also felt a deep need to disprove racist claims that blacks were only fit for slavery. In her *Narrative,* she refutes notions that Afro-Jamaicans would not work if free, and chronicles their hunger for religion and property, the pillars of civilization in the minds of her American readers. Even when her experiences with Jamaicans turn sour, she argues against a racial explanation. "It is not surprising that this people are full of deceit and lies," she writes, "this is the fruits of slavery, it makes masters and slaves knaves."

Nancy Prince had the misfortune to be in Jamaica when racial tensions began to take their toll on missionary activites, and she left the island in frustration.[9] The experience, nonetheless, confirmed her hostility to slavery and further encouraged her to commit her experiences to print. In 1841 she published a small pamphlet on Jamaica. Her *Narrative* first appeared in 1850, at a time when the debate over slavery in the United States was particularly intense. A second edition with some additional material—of which this is a reprint—appeared in 1853, and a third and final edition in 1856.

Whatever her intentions in writing her *Narrative*, Nancy Prince's story is almost as intriguing for what it does not say, or says elliptically, as for the wealth of adventure and description that she thought justified its publication. To be sure, she is open in expressing her rage and indignation at slavery and racism. Her words on those subjects are harsh and heartfelt. On other matters, nonetheless, near-silence prevails: she was a strong-minded woman reluctant to tell much about her personal life. The most striking example of her reticence is her failure to give her husband's first name, and the flat, sparse tone in which she writes about the marriage. Was, for example, her childlessness a relief or a sorrow? Did she grow to love the older man who took her away from the difficulties of her home life?

Equally interesting are her tantalizingly incomplete comments about religion and race. On the surface her Protestantism seems indistinguishable from that of thousands of her white contemporaries, but deeper in her *Narrative* lie glimpses of a black consciousness she may well have wished to conceal from her readership. Her mention of an African heritage is one such hint. She clearly admired her African grandfather and respected her harsh stepfather for his escape from a slave ship. The phrase she uses to describe each man—"stolen from Africa"—was common among abolitionists, but may well have had special meaning for a young girl who heard tales of a faraway homeland long before her baptism into Christianity. Even her Protestantism, similar as it sounds to white religion, may have had a racial consciousness that she did not care to reveal. She does not, for example, tell the reader that the Reverend Thomas Paul who baptized her was a leader among Boston's free blacks, active in the Masonic Lodge (as was her husband), and a founder of important institutions serving African-Americans. Among the latter was the Abyssinian Baptist Church in New York and his own church in Boston—presumably the one in which young Nancy Gardner was baptized and the first building in the city to be constructed entirely by black craftsmen.[10]

However "white" Nancy Prince may sound in her religious rhetoric and in her commitment to education and propriety, racial pride hovered in her background, long before it came to the forefront in her decision to journey to Jamaica. On the matter of racial injustice, of course, Nancy Prince could be outspoken and unsparing. Her vindication of Afro-Jamaicans in the face of racist slanders clearly drew upon a well-spring of personal experience and intense identification with them, in spite of great cultural differences. But when it comes to revealing her feelings about the emotional core of her life as an African-American woman, Prince draws a veil.

Perhaps that is as it should be and helps explain some of the fascination of her book. Any good story should have an element of mystery; the one at the center of Nancy Prince's *Narrative* is the author herself. A free-born African-American who painted vivid portraits of important moments in history and made keen observations of societies as different as Tsarist Russia and post-emancipation Jamaica, she leaves us wanting to know even more about the feisty, devoutly religious woman who saw it all.

Baltimore, August 1989

ENDNOTES

1. A useful guide to other autobiographical writings, some of which are listed in the bibliography at the end of this introduction, is Ann Allen Shockley, *Afro-American Women Writers, 1746–1933: An Anthology and Critical Guide* (Boston, 1988).

2. W. Jeffrey Bolster, " 'To Feel Like a Man': Black Seamen in the Northern States, 1800–1860," *Journal of American History* (forthcoming).

3. Dorothy Sterling, ed., *We Are Your Sisters: Black Women in the Nineteenth Century* (New York, 1984), p. 222; Elizabeth Cady Stanton, Susan B. Anthony, and Matilda Joslyn Gage, eds., *History of Woman Suffrage*, I (New York, 1881), p. 384.

4. Allison Blakely, *Russia and the Negro: Blacks in Russian History and Thought* (Washington, 1986), pp. 15–19.

5. William H. Grimshaw, *Official History of Freemasonry among the Colored People in North America* (New York, 1969 [originally published in 1903]), p. 98.

6. Blakely, *Russia and the Negro*, p. 18.

7. *Liberator*, March 8, 1839.

8. Philip D. Curtin, *Two Jamaicas: The Role of Ideas in a Tropical Colony, 1830–1865* (Cambridge, Mass., 1955), p. 162.

9. Curtin, *Two Jamaicas*, pp. 163–65.

10. Rayford W. Logan and Michael R. Winston, *Dictionary of American Negro Biography* (New York, 1982), pp. 482–83.

SELECT BIBLIOGRAPHY OF SOURCES USED

Andrews, William L., ed., *Sisters of the Spirit: Three Black Women's Autobiographies of the Nineteenth Century* (Bloomington, 1986).

Bell, Roseann P., Bettye J. Parker, and Beverly Guy-Sheftall, eds., *Sturdy Black Bridges: Visions of Black Women in Literature* (New York, 1979).

Billington, Ray Allen, *The Journal of Charlotte L. Forten: A Free Negro in the Slave Era* (New York, 1961).

Blakely, Allison, *Russia and the Negro: Blacks in Russian History and Thought* (Washington, 1986).

Bolster, W. Jeffrey, " 'To Feel Like a Man': Black Seamen in the Northern States, 1800–1860," *Journal of American History* (forthcoming).

Hine, Darlene Clark, "Lifting the Veil, Shattering the Silence: Black Women's History in Slavery and Freedom," in Darlene Clark Hine, ed., *The State of Afro-American History: Past, Present, and Future* (Baton Rouge, 1986).

Kolchin, Peter, *Unfree Labor: American Slavery and Russian Serfdom* (Cambridge, Mass., 1987).

Lerner, Gerda, ed., *Black Women in White America: A Documentary History* (New York, 1973).

Litwack, Leon F., *North of Slavery: The Negro in the Free States, 1790–1860* (Chicago, 1961).

Lowenberg, Bert James, and Ruth Bogin, eds., *Black Women in Nineteenth-Century American Life: Their Words, Their Thoughts, Their Feelings* (University Park, Penn., 1976).

Shockley, Ann Allen, *Afro-American Women Writers, 1746–1933: An Anthology and Critical Guide* (Boston, 1988).

Sterling, Dorothy, ed., *We Are Your Sisters: Black Women in the Nineteenth Century* (New York, 1984).

The Narrative
of
Nancy Prince

PREFACE

By divine aid, I attempt a second edition of my narrative, with the additions suggested to me by my friends. My object is not a vain desire to appear before the public; but, by the sale, I hope to obtain the means to supply my necessities. There are many benevolent societies for the support of Widows, but I am desirous not to avail myself of them, so long as I can support myself by my own endeavors. Infirmities are coming upon me, which induce me to solicit the patronage of my friends and the public, in the sale of this work. Not wishing to throw myself on them, I take this method to help myself, as health and strength are gone.

CONTENTS

NARRATIVE

I was born in Newburyport, September the 15th, 1799. My mother was born in Gloucester, Massachusetts—the daughter of Tobias Wornton, or Backus, so called. He was stolen from Africa, when a lad, and was a slave of Captain Winthrop Sargent; but, although a slave, he fought for liberty.[1] He was in the Revolutionary army, and at the battle of Bunker Hill. He often used to tell us, when little children, the evils of Slavery, and how he was stolen from his native land. My grandmother was an Indian of this country; she became a captive to the English, or their descendants. She served as a domestic in the Parsons family.[2] My father, Thomas Gardner, was born in Nantucket; his parents were of African descent. He died in Newburyport, when I was three months old. My mother was thus a second time left a widow, with her two children, and she returned to Gloucester to her father. My mother married her third husband, by whom she had six children. My stepfather was stolen from

Africa, and while the vessel was at anchor in
one of our Eastern ports, he succeeded in making his escape from his captors, by swimming
ashore. I have often heard him tell the tale.
Having some knowledge of the English language, he found no trouble to pass. There
were two of them, and they found, from observation, that they were in a free State. I have
heard my father describe the beautiful moon-
light night when they two launched their
bodies into the deep, for liberty. When they got
upon soundings, their feet were pricked with a
sea-plant that grew under water, they had to
retreat, and, at last they reached the shore.
When day began to break, they laid down
under a fence, as naked as they were born—
soon they heard a rattling sound, and trembling, they looked to see what it meant. In a
few minutes, a man with a broad-brimed hat
on, looked over the fence and cried out, "Hal-
loo boys! you are from that ship at anchor?"
Trembling, we answered, yes. He kindly took
us by the hand, and told us not to fear, for we
were safe. "Jump, boys," said he, "into my
cart," which we readily did. He turned about,
and soon entered a large yard—we were taken
to his house and carried to an apartment,
where he brought us clothes and food, and
cheered us with every kindness. No search
was made for us; it was supposed we were
drowned, as many had jumped over-board on
the voyage, thinking they could get home to

Africa again. I have often heard my step-father boast how brave they were, and say they stood like men and saw the ship set sail with less than half they stole from Africa. He was selling his bamboo baskets, when he was seized by white men, and put in a boat, and taken on board the ship that lay off; many such ships there were! He was called "Money Vose," and his name may be found on the Custom House books in Gloucester. His last voyage was with Captain Elias Davis, in the brig Romulus, belonging to Captain Fitz William Sargent, in whose employ he had been twelve years. During the war, the brig was taken by a British privateer, and he was pressed into their service. He was sick with the dropsy a long while, and died oppressed, in the English dominions. My mother was again left a widow, with an infant six weeks old, and seven other children. When she heard of her husband's death, she exclaimed, "I thought it; what shall I do with these children?" She was young, inexperienced, with no hope in God, and without the knowledge of her Saviour. Her grief, poverty, and responsibilities, were too much for her; she never again was the mother that she had been before. I was, at this time, in Captain F. W. Sargent's family. I shall never forget the feelings I experienced, on hearing of the decease of my father-in-law,[3] although he was not kind to me or my sister; but, by industry a humble home was provided, for my mother and her younger children. Death had twice visited our family, in less than three months. My grandfather died before my father-in-law sailed. I thought I would go home a little while, and try and comfort my mother. The three oldest children were put into families.

My brother and myself stayed at home that Summer. We gathered berries and sold them in Gloucester; strawberries; raspberries, black-berries and whortleberries, were in abun-dance, in the stony environs, growing spon-taneously. With the sale of these fruits, my brother and myself nearly supported my mother and her children, that Summer. My brother George, young as he was, caught fish and sold them, and run of errands, and was always watching for something to do, that he might help his mother. At one time he was missing; we expected he was drowned; a search was made for him in the water; the neighbors were all on the alert. Poor mother returning from a hard day's work, supposing the boy was lost, was like a lunatic. The lad was supposed to have fallen from the wharf, where he was fishing. Our friends had all given up the search—it was then eleven o'clock at night. Mother and I locked up the children and went round to the harbor, to one Captain Warner, who traded to the Eastward. Mrs. Warner in-formed us that my brother came there in the morning, with his bundle, and they supposed he was sent, as the Captain wished to take him with him. He went on board, and the vessel sailed that afternoon. In three weeks, he came home, to the comfort of his mother and all of us. He brought back, for his pay, four feet of wood and three dollars.

We stayed with our mother until every resource was exhausted; we then heard of a place eight miles out of town, where a boy and girl were wanted. We both went and were engaged. We often went home with our wages, and all the comforts we could get; but we could not approach our mother as we wished. God in mercy took one little boy of seven years, who had been in a consumption one year.

My oldest sister, Silvia, was seventy miles in the country, with the family that brought her up; so we were scattered all about. Soon as the war was over, I determined to get more for my labor. I left Essex and went to Salem, in the month of April, 1814, without a friend, without a guide. I first went to Gloucester, to bid my mother and the family adieu. George, my brother, I left with a promise to send for him when I should be settled. When I reached the Cove, about five miles from Gloucester, I stopped at a friend's, who urged me not to go, holding up obstacles. It rained and snowed, but I travelled along, following the guide-posts, until I reached Beverly bridge. I crossed it when the clock struck four, in the afternoon. I now wished to find a friend in Becket Street, Salem, but was afraid of the people that I met near the Bridge, they were so covered with rags and dirt. I kept on until I reached the Common; I then asked a woman who was neatly dressed, for the lady I wished to find. She did not know. I asked for another person that I knew was not very good; she took me there, but I soon found my friend that I wished, and stopped there two weeks, and then went to live with a respectable colored family. My mother was not satisfied, and came after me. I would not go to Gloucester. She left me at a friend's, and this woman had a daughter, who came home from service, sick. I took her place, and thought myself fortunate to be with religious people, as I had enjoyed the happy privilege of religious instruction. My dear grandfather was a member of a Congregational Church, and a good man; he always attended meeting in the morning, and took his children with him. In the afternoon he took care of the smaller children, while my mother attended with her little group. He thought it was wrong for us to go to school where the teacher was not devoted to God. Thus I early knew the difference between right and wrong.

There were seven in the family, one sick with a fever, and another in a consumption; and of course, the work must have been very severe, especially the washings. Sabbath evening I had to prepare for the wash; soap the clothes and put them into the steamer, set the kettle of water to boiling, and then close in the steam, and let the pipe from the boiler into the steam box that held the clothes. At two o'clock, on the morning of Monday, the bell was rung for me to get up; but, that was not all, they said I was too slow, and the washing was not done well; I had to leave the tub to tend the door and wait on the family, and was not spoken kind to, at that.

Hard labor and unkindness was too much for me; in three months, my health and strength were gone. I often looked at my employers, and thought to myself, is this your religion? I did not wonder that the girl who had lived there previous to myself, went home to die. They had family prayers, morning and evening. Oh! yes, they were sanctimonious! I was a poor stranger, but fourteen years of age, imposed upon by these good people; but I must leave them. In the year 1814, they sent me to Gloucester in their chaise. I found my poor mother in bad health, and I was sick also; but, by the mercy of God, and the attention and skill of Dr. Dale, and the kindness of friends, I was restored, so that in a few months, I was able to go to work, although my side afflicted me, which I attributed to overworking myself.

In the Spring of 1815, I returned to Salem, accompanied by my eldest sister, and we obtained good places. She took it into her head to go to Boston, as a nursery girl, where she lived a few months and was then deluded away.

February 7th, 1816, a friend came to Salem and
informed me of it. To have heard of her death,
would not have been so painful to me, as we
loved each other very much, and more particularly, as our step-father was not very kind
to us. When little girls, she used to cry about
it, and we used to say, when were were large
enough we would go away.

It was very cold; but notwithstanding, I was
so distressed about my sister that I started the
next morning for Boston, on foot. A friend was
with me. At Lynn Hotel we refreshed ourselves, and all seemed much interested about
me; two women took me aside, and inquired
how it was that I was with that woman. I told
my reason; she was well known all about; she
lived as a cook in Boston, she came after her
son, a little child whom she held in her arms.
By the time we were seven miles from Salem,
cold and fatigued, I could walk no farther, and
we hired a horse and sleigh, and a man to
drive us to Boston, where we arrived at seven
o'clock in the evening. The house where we
stopped was in Green street, the lady kindly
invited me to stop; I refused; I was suspicious
the house was not good; the woman I came
with took me to Belknap street, where I found
an old friend; I would not stop, they went with
me to Bedford street, where I intended to put
up. The inmates received me very kindly; my
feet, hands and ears were all frostbitten. I
needed all the hospitality that was extended to

me. I was young and inexperienced, but God knew that my object was good. "In wisdom he chooses the weak things of the earth." Without his aid, how could I ever have rescued my lost sister? Mr. Brown, when he learned my errand, kindly offered to assist me. He found where my sister resided, and taking with him a large cane, he accompanied me to the house, on Sabbath evening. My sister I found seated with a number of others round a fire, the mother of harlots at the head. My sister did not see me until I clasped her round the neck. The old woman flew at me, and bid me take my hands off of her; she opened a door that led down into a cellar kitchen, and told me to come down, she attempted to take my hands off of my sister. Mr. Brown defended me with his cane; there were many men and girls there, and all was confusion. When my sister came to herself, she looked upon me and said: "Nancy, O Nancy, I am ruined!" I said, "Silvia, my dear sister, what are you here for? Will you not go with me?" She seemed thankful to get away; the enraged old woman cried out, "she owes me, she cannot go." Silvia replied, "I will go." The old woman seized her to drag her down into the kitchen; I held on to her, while Mr. Brown at my side, used his great cane; he threatened her so that she was obliged to let my sister go, who, after collecting her things, accompanied Mr. Brown and myself.

Now while I write, I am near the spot that

that was then the hold of all foul and unclean things. "The lips of a strange woman drop as an honey comb, and her mouth is smoother than oil; there she has slain her thousands; her end is bitter as wormwood, sharp as a two-edged sword, and lieth in wait at every corner, with an impudent face, saying, I have peace offerings, I have payed my vows. With her much fair speech, she flattereth: she hath cast down many wounded, yea, many strong have been slain by her; her house is the way to hell going down to the chambers of death." Even now, I cannot refrain my feelings, although death has long separated us; but her soul is precious; she was very dear to me; she was five years older than myself, and often protected me from the blows of an unkind step-father. She often said she was not fit to live, nor fit to die.

The next day, after breakfast, one of Mrs. Brown's daughters accompanied us to the stage office; we expected Mr. Low, the driver of the Gloucester stage, who knew us as his towns-people, would let us take passage with him without any difficulty; but he refused unless we would ride upon the top. It was very cold; I had sent my mother my wages the week before, and what money I had, I had taken in advance, of my employers. We were greatly embarrassed, when a colored man, unknown to us, penetrated our difficulty, and asked us if we had two dollars; we told him we had; he very kindly took us to the stage office, and we bargained for a horse and sleigh to carry us to Salem, where we arrived safely in about two hours and a half; and we gave up our conveyance to the same owners, with ten thousand thanks to our colored friend, and to our Heavenly Father; had we attempted to walk, we must have frozen by the way. The horse and sleigh belonged to the stage-office, so we had no more care for that. The man who let it to us was very humane, although a stranger. The price was two dollars, of which he not only gave us back fifty cents to pay our toll, but went with us as far as to Charlestown bridge.

I often thought of the contrast between our townsman, Mr. Low, and the stranger who was so kind to us. The lady I lived with, Mrs. John Deland, received us very kindly, and permitted my sister to remain with me awhile; then she returned to Gloucester, to the family who brought her up, and I thought we had gained a great victory.

My brother George and myself were very desirous to make our mother comfortable: he went to sea for that purpose; the next April, I came to Boston to get a higher price for my labor; for we had agreed to support my mother, and hoped she would take home our little brother and take care of him, who was supported by the town. George came home, and sailed again in the same employ, leaving mother a draw bill for half his wages. My sister returned to Boston to find me, and wished to procure a place to work out. I had just changed my place for one more retired, and engaged my sister with me as a chamber maid; she tried me much. I thought it a needy time, for I had not yielded my heart to the will of God, though I had many impressions, and formed many resolutions; but the situations that I had been placed in, (having left my mother's house at the age of eight,) had not permitted me to do as I wished, although the kind counsels of my dear grandfather and pious teachers followed me wherever I went. Care after care oppressed me—my mother wandered about like a Jew— the young children who were in families were dissatisfied; all hope but in God was lost. I resolved, in my mind, to seek an interest in my Savior, and put my trust in Him; and never shall I forget the place or time when God spake to my troubled conscience. Justified by faith I found peace with God, the forgiveness of sin through Jesus Christ my Lord. After living sixteen years without hope, and without a guide, May 6th, 1819, the Rev. Thomas Paul, baptized myself, and seven others in obedience to the great command.

> We, on him our anchor cast—
> Poor and needy, lean on him,
> He will bring us through at last.

The same day, we received the right hand of fellowship from our then beloved pastor. After the absence of nine years, I had the happy privilege of meeting with two of the number, who were unshaken in the faith; they have since gone to join the spirits in glory. I had the happy privilege of attending them in sickness.

I now turn to the scenes of youth. George again returned home, and we again provided a home for mother and the little ones. He shipped in the same vessel again, and affairs now seemed to promise comfort and respectability; but mother chose to marry again; this was like death to us all. George returned home, but was so disappointed that he shipped again to return no more. Although a boy of sixteen, he was as steady as most men at twenty. My cares were consequently increased, having no one to share them with me. My next brother, who lived in South Essex, came to Salem to his mother's, but was driven away by her husband, and came to me; I carried him to Gloucester and left him in the hands of the town; he stayed but three weeks, and returned to me again; I then boarded him out for one dollar a week, until I could procure suitable employment for him. When winter came, poor mother's health was declining. Little Samuel could do but little; my father-in-law was very cross, his disappointment was very great, for he expected to be supported by my brother George and myself. I could not see my mother suffer, therefore I left my place and went to Salem to watch over her and Samuel, and lived in the Rev. Dr. Bolle's family. In the

Spring, I returned to Boston, and took my brother Samuel with me; soon after, my sister Lucy left her place and went to her mother, but was not permitted to stay; my mother wrote to me, requesting me to take care of her. I then determined, in my mind, to bring her to Boston, and if possible, procure a place for her; I then had Samuel and John on my hands; Lucy was not nine, and very small of her age, I could not easily get her a place, but fortunately obtained board for her and Samuel for one dollar a week. My brother John, whom I had boarded, at last got a place where he had wages. Soon the Lord opened the way for little Samuel; Dr. Phelps took him to bring up: so that I was left with one only to sustain; soon my hopes were blasted. John left his place, and was several months on my hands again; finally, he made up his mind to go to sea; I was so thankful that he had concluded to do something, that I took two months' wages in advance to fit him out for Liverpool, in five months he returned without a single thing but the clothes he had on. The ship brought passengers from Ireland. As soon as the vessel arrived, he came to seek me; I went with him for his things; but passengers and all were gone. His wages were small, not enough to make him comfortable: and, had not a friend given him a home, he would again have been dependent on my exertions; another friend took Lucy, with whom she stayed eleven months. She lived in different families until she was about twelve years old; I then put her in the Rev. Mr. Mann's family, at Westminister, for a certain time, thinking it would be best for her; and John I left to fight his own battles. My sister Silvia, was one of my greatest trials. Knowing she was in Boston, my mother, in one of her spells of insanity, got away from her home and travelled to Boston after her; she came where I lived, my employers were very kind to her, she tarried a few days, when I hired a horse and chaise and took them both back to Salem, and returned to my place in 1822, with a determination to do something for myself; I left my place after three months, and went to learn a trade; and after seven years of anxiety and toil, I made up my mind to leave my country. September 1st, 1823, Mr. Prince arrived from Russia. February 15th, 1824, we were married. April 14th, we embarked on board the Romulus, captain Epes Sargent commander, bound for Russia. May 24th, arrived at Elsinore, left the same day for Copenhagen, where we remained twelve days. We visited the king's palace, and several other extensive and beautiful buildings. We attended a number of entertainments, among the Danes and English, who were religious; observed that their manners and customs were similar; they are attentive to strangers; the Sabbath is very strictly observed; the principal religion is Lutheran and Calvinistic, but all persuasions are tolerated. The languages are Dutch, French and English. The Danes are very modest and kind, but like all other nations, they know how to take the advantage. We left Copenhagen the 7th of June, and arrived at Cronstadt on the 19th; left there the 21st for St. Petersburg, and in a few hours, were happy to find ourselves at our place of destination, through the blessing of God, in good health, and soon made welcome from all quarters. We took lodgings with a Mrs. Robinson, a native of our country, who was Patience Mott, of Providence, who left here in the year 1813, in the family of Alexander Gabriel, the man who was taken for Mr. Prince. There I spent six weeks very pleasantly, visiting and receiving friends, in the manner of the country. While there I attended two of their parties; there were various amusements in which I did not partake, which caused them much disappointment. I told them my religion did not allow of dancing or dice playing, which formed part of the amusements. As they were very strict in their religion, they indulged me in the same privilege. By the help of God I was ever enabled to preserve my stand.

Mr. Prince was born in Marlborough, and lived in families in this city. In 1810 he went to Gloucester, and sailed with captain Theodore Stanwood, for Russia. He returned with him and remained in his family, and at this time visited at my mother's. He sailed with captain Stanwood in 1812, for the last time. The Captain took with him his son Theodore, in order to place him in School in St. Petersburg. When the Captain sailed for home, Mr. Price went to serve the Princess Purtossof, one of the noble ladies of the Court. The palace where the imperial family reside is called the court, or the seat of Government. This magnificent building is adorned with all the ornaments that possibly can be explained; there are hundreds of people that inhabit it, besides the soldiers that guard it. There are several of these splendid edifices in the city and vicinity. The one that I was presented in, was in a village, three miles from the city. After leaving the carriage, we entered the first ward; where the usual salutation by the guards was performed. As we passed through the beautiful hall, a door was opened by two colored men in official dress. The Emperor Alexander, stood on his throne, in his royal apparel. The throne is circular, elevated two steps from the floor, and covered with scarlet velvet, tasseled with gold; as I entered, the Emperor stepped forward with great politeness and condescension, and welcomed me, and asked several questions; he then accompanied us to the Empress Elizabeth; she stood in her dignity, and received me in the same manner the Emperor had. They presented me with a watch, &c. It was customary in those days, when any one married, belonging to the court, to present them with gifts, according to their standard; there was no prej-

udice against color; there were all casts, and
the people of all nations, each in their place.

The number of colored men that filled this
station was twenty; when one dies, the
number is immediately made up. Mr. Prince
filled the place of one that had died. They serve
in turns, four at a time, except on some great
occasions, when all are employed. Provision is
made for the families within or without the
palace. Those without go to court at 8 o'clock
in the morning; after breakfasting, they take
their station in the halls, for the purpose of
opening the doors, at signal given, when the
Emperor and Empress pass.

First of August, we visited the burying-
ground where the people meet, as they say, to
pay respect to their dead. It is a great holiday;
they drink and feast on the grave stones, or as
near the grave as they can come; some groan
and pray, and some have music and dancing.
At a funeral no one attends except the invited;
after the friends arrive, a dish of rice, boiled
hard, with raisins, is handed round; all are to
take a spoonful, with the same spoon, and out
of the same dish; in the meanwhile the priest,
with his clerk, performs the ceremony, per-
fuming the room with incense. The lid is not
put on to the coffin, the corpse being laid out
in his or her best dress. The torch-men (who
are dressed in black garments, made to slope
down to their feet, with broad brimmed hats
that cover their shoulders,) form a procession,

with lighted torches in their hands, bowing
their heads as they pass along very gravely;
then comes one more with the lid on his head;
then the hearse with the corpse drawn by four
horses, covered with black gowns down to
their feet; they all move along with great sol-
emnity. Before entering the grave-yard, the
procession goes to an adjoining church, where
there are many ladies, placed on benches, side
by side, according to their ages; the ladies
dressed as if they were going to a ball-room,
displaying a most dreadful appearance. Each
one has her hands crossed, and holding in one
of them a pass to give to Peter, that they may
enter into Heaven. At this place they light their
candles, and receive their rice in the manner
before mentioned. The top is then put on to
the coffin, and the procession forms and re-
pairs to the grave; the priest sanctifies the
grave, then casts in dust, and the coffin is
consigned to its narrow-house; then com-
mence the yells; they drink, eat cake, black
bread, and finish their rice, when the party
return back to dinner, where every thing has
been prepared during their absence. This is the
Greek mode of burying their dead. On the
birth of a child, the babe is not dressed until it
is baptized; it is immersed all over in water; a
stand with an oval basin, is brought for the
purpose by the clerk. The mother is presented
with gifts, which are placed under her pillow.
Should the babe die before this rite is per-

formed, it is not placed with the others; but should it die having been baptized, although not more than two hours old, it is dressed and placed on the bench at church with the rest. In this manner, the common people bury their dead.

When any of the imperial family dies, they are laid in state forty days, and every thing accordingly. There is a building built expressly for the imperial families, where their remains are deposited. In the front part of it, the criminals that have rebelled against the imperial family are placed in cells, thus combining the prison and the tomb; and in sailing by, these miserable creatures are exposed to the careless gaze of unfeeling observers.

St. Petersburg was inundated October 9th, 1824. The water rose sixteen feet in most parts of the city; many of the inhabitants were drowned. An island between the city and Cronstadt, containing five hundred inhabitants, was inundated, and all were drowned, and great damage was done at Cronstadt. The morning of this day was fair; there was a high wind. Mr. Prince went early to the palace, as it was his turn to serve; our children boarders were gone to school; our servant had gone of an errand. I heard a cry, and to my astonishment, when I looked out to see what was the matter, the waters covered the earth. I had not then learned the language, but I beckoned to the people to come in. The waters continued to rise until 10 o'clock, A.M. The waters were then within two inches of my window, when they ebbed and went out as fast as they had come in, leaving to our view a dreadful sight. The people who came into my house for their safety retired, and I was left alone. At four o'clock in the afternoon, there was darkness that might be felt, such as I had never experienced before. My situation was the more painful, being alone, and not being able to speak. I waited until ten in the evening; I then took a lantern, and started to go to a neighbor's, whose children went to the same school with my boarders. I made my way through a long yard, over the bodies of men and beasts, and when opposite their gate I sunk; I made one grasp, and the earth gave away; I grasped again, and fortunately got hold of the leg of a horse, that had been drowned. I drew myself up, covered with mire, and made my way a little further, when I was knocked down by striking against a boat, that had been washed up and left by the retiring waters; and as I had lost my lantern, I was obliged to grope my way as I could, and feeling along the walk, I at last found the door that I aimed at. My family were safe and they accompanied me home. At 12 o'clock, Mr. Prince came home, as no one was permitted to leave the palace, till his majesty had viewed the city. In the morning the children and the girl returned, and I went to view the pit into which I had sunk. It was large enough to hold a dozen like myself, where the earth had caved in. Had not the horse been there, I should never again have seen the light of day, and no one would have known my fate. Thus through the providence of God, I escaped from the flood and the pit.

> My helper, God, I bless thy name;
> The same thy power, thy grace the same;
> I 'midst ten thousand dangers stand,
> Supported by thy guardian hand."

Should I attempt to give an account of all the holidays, it would fill volumes. The next to notice is Christmas and New Year. The first day of January a grand masquerade is given by his majesty, at the winter palace; forty thousand tickets are distributed; every thing is done in order; every gentleman wears a mask and cloak, and carries a lady with him. They are formed in a procession, and enter at the west gate; as they pass through, all the golden vessels and ornaments are displayed; these were back of a counter, which extends two hundred feet; there the company receive a cup of hot chocolate, and a paper of comfits, and a bun; a great many are in attendance, as a vast many persons are permitted to pass in and view the palace, and go out at the east gate.

The 6th of January is a still greater day, for then the water is christened; a church is built on the ice, ornamented with gold and evergreens, and a row of spruce trees, extending from the door of the palace to the church. At this time all the nobles, of different nations, make their appearance in their native costume. The Patriarch, Archbishops, and other dignitaries of the court, have a service; then they pass through and christen the water, and make it holy; then there is a great rush of the people for this holy water. On the plain an ice hill is built, eighty feet high, where the emperor and his court exercise themselves.

February 10th is another holiday. Buildings are constructed on the plain for the occasion. All kinds of amusements may be found here, and all kinds of animals seen; much time and money are spent. The buildings are built in rotation. All the children of the different seminaries and institutions of education, are driven round in gilded carriages to witness the performances. After this is the great Fast, previous to the crucifixion of our Saviour. Then Christ is represented as riding into Jerusalem; branches of trees are placed on the ice, and strewed through the streets, and every performance is carried out. The Saviour is made of white marble; he is crucified and buried, and on the third day he rises, according to the Scriptures; then the cannons are fired. At the close of this forty day's Fast, they have a great feast and fair; all business is suspended, and the festivity and frolic continue for one week.

The first day of May is another great holiday. The merchant's daughters are arranged on each side of a long mall, in the beautiful gardens, and arrayed in their best clothes, under the care of an old woman known in their families; the gentlemen walk round and observe them, and if they see one they fancy, they speak to the old woman; she takes him to the parents and introduces him; if the parties agree, they prepare for the betrothal. It is their custom to marry one of their own station. All these holidays are accounted sacred. The first year I noted them all, as I was accustomed to attend them.

May, 1825. I spent some time visiting the different towns in the vicinity of St. Petersburg. In the fall of the same year, the Emperor retired to a warmer climate for the health of the Empress Elizabeth. January, 1826, the corpse of Alexander was brought in state, and was met three miles from the city by the nobles of the court; and they formed a procession, and the body was brought in state into the building where the imperial family were deposited. March, of the same year, the corpse of Elizabeth was brought in the same manner. Constantine was then king of Poland, he was next heir to the throne, and was, unanimously voted by the people, but refused and resigned the crown in favor of his brother Nicholas. The day appointed the people were ordered to assemble as usual, at the ringing of the bells; they rejected Nicholas; a sign was given by the leaders that was well understood, and the people great and small rushed to the square and cried with one voice for Constantine. The emperor with his prime minister, and city governor, rode into the midst of them, entreating them to retire, without avail; they were obliged to order the cannons fired upon the mob; it was not known when they discharged them that the emperor and his ministers were in the crowd. He was wonderfully preserved, while both his friends and their horses were killed. There was a general seizing of all classes, who were taken into custody. The scene cannot be described; the bodies of the killed and mangled were cast into the river, and the snow and ice were stained with the blood of human victims; as they were obliged to drive the cannon to and fro in the midst of the crowd, the bones of those wounded, who might have been cured, were crushed. The cannon are very large, drawn by eight horses, trained for the purpose. The scene was awful; all business was stopped. This deep plot originated in 1814, in Germany, with the Russian nobility and German, under the pretence of a Free Mason's Lodge. When they returned home they increased their numbers and presented their chart to the emperor for permission, which was granted. In the year 1822, the emperor being suspicious that all was not right, took their chart from them. They carried it on in small parties, rapidly increasing, believing they would soon be able to destroy all the imperial branches, and have a republican government. Had not this take place, undoubtedly they would at last have succeeded. So deep was the foundation of this plot laid, both males and females were engaged in it. The prison-houses were filled, and thirty of the leading men were put in solitary confinement, and twenty-six of the number died, four were burned. A stage was erected and faggots were placed underneath, each prisoner was secured by iron chains, presenting a most appalling sight to an eye-witness. A priest was in attendance to cheer their last dying moments, then fire was set to the faggots, and those brave men were consumed. Others received the knout, and even the princesses and ladies of rank were imprisoned and flogged in their own habitations. Those that survived their punishment were banished to Siberia. The mode of banishment is very imposing and very heart-rending, severing them from all dear relatives and friends, for they are never permitted to take their children. When they arrive at the gate of the city, their first sight is a guard of soldiers, then wagons with provisions, then the noblemen in their banished apparel guarded, then each side, conveyances for the females, then ladies in order, guarded by soldiers.

Preparations were now being made for the coronation of the new Emperor and Empress. This took place September, 1826, in Moscow, 555 miles south-east from St. Petersburg. All persons engaged in the court were sent beforehand, in order to prepare for the coming event. After his majesty's laws were read, as usual on such occasions, those who wished to remain in his service did so, and those who did not were discharged.

After the coronation, the Emperor and his court returned to St. Petersburg. June, 1827, war was declared between Russia and Turkey. They had several battles, with varied success. The Russians surrounded and laid siege to Constantinople. The Sultan of Turkey sued for peace, and a treaty was at last signed, and peace was proclaimed in 1829. In March, of the same year, war was declared with Poland. 1831. The cholera, that malignant disease, made its appearance in Austria, from thence to little Russia, making great ravages, thousands of people falling a prey. It then began to rage in St. Petersburg, carrying off 9255. This disease first appeared in Madagascar, 1814, where most of the inhabitants died. It is called the plague, that God sent among the people of Israel and other nations, for centuries back. Much might be said of this dreadful disease and others that are but little known in this country. God often visits nations, families, and persons, with judgments as well as mercies.[4]

The present Emperor and Empress are courteous and affable. The Empress would often send for the ladies of the court at 8 oclock in the evening to sup with her: when they arrive at the court they form a procession and she takes the lead. On entering the hall, the band strikes up; there are two long tables on each side, and in the midst circular tables for the Imperial family. The tables are spread apparently with every variety of eatables and desserts, but everything is artificial, presenting a novel appearance. When the company are seated, the Emperor and Empress walk around the tables and shake hands with each individual, as they pass. The prisoners of war who are nobles, are seated by themselves with their faces veiled. There is a tender or waiter to each person, with two plates, one with soup and the other with something else. After a variety of courses, in one hour they are dismissed by the band. They then retire to another part of the palace to attend a ball or theatrical amusements. At the Empress' command they are dismissed. She carries power and dignity in her countenance, and is well adapted to her station. And after her late amusements at night, she would be out at an early hour in the morning, visiting the abodes of the distressed, dressed in as common apparel as any one here, either walking, or riding in a common sleigh. At her return she would call for her children, to take them in her arms and talk to them. "She riseth while it is yet night and giveth meat to her household and a portion to her maidens, she stretcheth out her hands to the poor, yea, she reacheth out her hands to the needy; she is not afraid of the snow, for all her household are clothed in scarlet." Then she would go to the cabinet of his Majesty; there she would write and advise with him.

The Russian ladies follow the fashions of the French and English. Their religion is after the Greek Church. There are no seats in their churches; they stand, bow, and kneel, during the service. The principal church is on the Main street. There are the statues of the great commanders that have conquered in battle. They are clad in brass, with flags in their hands, and all their ancient implements of war are deposited there. The altar is surrounded by statues of the Virgin Mary and the twelve apostles. When Russia is at war, and her armies are about to engage in battle, it is here that the Emperor and his family and court, come to pray for victory over the enemy. The day they engaged in battle against the Poles, the Empress Dowager took her death; she was embalmed and laid in state six weeks in the hall of the winter palace. I went a number of times to see her, and the people pay her homage, and kiss the hands of that lump of clay. All religion is tolerated, but the native Russians are subject to the Greek Church. There are a number of institutions in St. Petersburg where children of all classes have the privilege of instruction. The sailors' and soldiers' boys enter the corps at the age of seven, and are educated for that purpose. The girls remain in the barracks with their parents, or go to some institution where they are instructed in all the branches of female education. There are other establishments, where the higher classes send their children.

There is another spacious building called the Market, half a mile square, where all kinds of articles may be bought. Between the Market and the church there is a block of buildings where silver articles of all kinds are to be purchased. These stores present a very superb appearance and are visited by every foreigner that comes into the place. Besides these buildings, Main Street is lined with elegant buildings with projecting windows, to the extent of twelve miles. Nearly at the termination of the street there is a spacious building of stone which encloses the Taberisey Garden, so called from its having every kind of tree, shrub, flower and fruit, of the known world, which flourish alike in winter as in summer. There is an extensive Frozen Market which forms a square as large as Boston Common. This space of ground is covered with counters, on which may be purchased every variety of eatable, such as frozen fish, fowl, and meats of every description, besides every other article of commerce which will bear the extreme cold of a St. Petersburg winter. This city was founded by Peter the Great, and built upon a bog which was occupied by a few fishermen's huts, and belonged to the Finns. It is situated at the extremity of the Gulf of Finland, and is built partly on the main land and partly on several small islands. The foundation of the city is extremely marshy, which subjects it to frequent inundations. For this reason there are canals which are cut through the streets, very beautifully laid out, faced with granite, railed with iron chains nubbed with brass, with bridges to cross from one street to the other. The city houses are built of stone and brick, and twice the thickness of American houses. They are heated by Peaches, of similar construction to our furnaces; the outside of which is faced with China tiles, presenting a very beautiful appearance. The village houses are built of logs corked with oakum, where the peasants reside. This class of people till the land, most of them are slaves and are very degraded.[5] The rich own the poor, but they are not suffered to separate families or sell them off the soil. All are subject to the Emperor, and no nobleman can leave without his permission. The mode of travelling is principally by stages which are built something like our omnibusses, with settees upon the top railed and guarded by soldiers, for the purpose of protecting the travellers from the attacks of wild beasts. The common language is a mixture of Sclavonian and Polish. The nobility make use of the modern Greek, French and English. I learned the languages in six months, so as to be able to attend to my business, and also made some proficiency in the French. My time was taken up in domestic affairs; I took two children to board, the third week after commencing housekeeping, and increased their numbers. The baby linen making and childrens' garments were in great demand. I started a business in these articles and took a journeywoman and apprentices. The present Empress is a very active one, and inquired of me respecting my business, and gave me much encouragement by purchasing of me garments for herself and children, handsomely wrought in French and English styles, and many of the nobility also followed her example. It was to me a great blessing that we had the means of grace afforded us. The Rev. Richard Kennell, was the Protestant pastor. We had service twice every Sabbath, and evening prayer meetings, also a female society, so that I was occupied at all times.

At the time of the inundation, the Bibles and other books belonging to the society were injured. But Mr. Kenell took the liberty to purchase at full price and sell at an advance. In order that the poor might have them, we all agreed to labor for that purpose. I often visited the matron of the Empress' children, and encouraged by her I took some to the Palace, and by this means disposed of many at head quarters. Other friends without the court continued to labor until hundreds and thousands were disposed of. The old Bishop finding his

Kronstadt, the Port of St. Petersburg

Winter Palace in St. Petersburg, Residence of the Imperial Family

The Great Flood of 1824

Punishment of the "Knout"

Frozen Provision Market, St. Petersburg

City Amusements "Mountains of Ice"

Kingston in the Nineteenth Century

Metropolitan School in Early Nineteenth-Century Jamaica

Interior of a Jamaican Baptist Church

Visit of a Missionary to a Plantation Village

Cane-Cutting in Early Nineteenth-Century Jamaica

Spanish Town, the Proclamation of the Emancipation, 1834

religion was in danger sent a petition to the Emperor that all who were found distributing Bibles and Tracts should be punished severely. Many were taken and imprisoned, two devoted young men were banished; thus the righteous were punished, while evil practices were not forbidden, for there the sin of licentiousness is very common.

I have mentioned that the climate did not agree with me; in winter my lungs were much affected. It was the advice of the best physicians that I had better not remain in Russia during another cold season. However painful it was to me to return without my husband, yet life seemed desirable, and he flattered me and himself that he should soon follow. It is difficult for any one in the Emperor's employment to leave when they please. Mr. Prince thought it best for me to return to my native country, while he remained two years longer to accumulate a little property, and then return— but death took him away. I left St. Petersburg, August 14th, 1833, having been absent about nine years and six months. On the 17th, I sailed from Cronstadt, for New York. Arrived at Elsinore the 25th. Tuesday, 29, left. September the 2d, laid to in a gale. September 18th, made Plymouth, Old England, 19th sailed. Arrived in New York, Oct. 10th. Left there Tuesday 18th, arrived in Boston the 23d. Sabbath, Nov. 9th, I had the privilege of attending service in the old place of worship. On this day I also had the pleasure of meeting with an old friend of my grandfather, nearly one hundred years of age. I found things much changed; my mother and sister Silvia died in 1827, (that I was aware of.) The Rev. T. Paul was dead, and many of my old friends were gone to their long home. The old church and society was in much confusion; I attempted to worship with them but it was in vain. The voyage was of great benefit to me. By the advice of friends I applied to a Mrs. Mott, a female physician in the city, that helped me much.[6] I am indebted to God for his great goodness in guiding my youthful steps; my mind was directed to my fellow brethren whose circumstances were similar to my own. I found many a poor little orphan destitute and afflicted, and on account of color shut out from all the asylums for poor children. At this my heart was moved, and I proposed to my friends the necessity of a home for such, where they might be sheltered from the contaminating evils that beset their path. For this purpose I called a meeting of the people and laid before them my plan: as I had had the privilege of assisting in forming an Asylum for such a purpose in St. Petersburg, I thought it would be well to establish one on the same principles, not knowing that any person had had a thought of anything of the kind. We commenced with eight children. I gave three months of my time. A board was formed of seven females, with a commitee of twelve gentlemen of standing, to superintend. At the end of three months the committee was dispensed with, and for want of funds our society soon fell through.

I passed my time in different occupations and making arrangements for the return of my husband, but death took him from me. I made my home at the Rev. J. W. Holman's, a Free Will Baptist, until I sailed for Jamaica. There had been an Anti-Slavery Society established by W. L. Garrison, Knapp, and other philanthropists of the day. Their design was the amelioration of the nominally free colored people of these States, and the emancipation of the slaves in other States. These meetings I attended with much pleasure, until a contention broke out among themselves; there has been a great change in some things, but much remains to be done; possibly I may not see so clearly as some, for the weight of prejudice has again oppressed me, and were it not for the promises of God, one's heart would fail, for *He* made man in his own image, in the image of God, created he him, male and female, that they should have dominion over the fish of the sea, the fowl of the air, and the beast of the field, &c. This power did God give man, that thus far should he go and no farther; but man has disobeyed his Maker, and become vain in his imagination, and their foolish hearts are darkened. We gather from this, that God has in all ages of the world punished every nation

and people for their sins. The sins of my beloved country are not hid from his notice; his
all seeing eye sees and knows the secrets of all
hearts; the angels that kept not their first estate
but left their own habitations, he hath reserved
in everlasting chains unto the great day.

My mind, after the emancipation in the West
Indies, was bent upon going to Jamaica. A field
of usefulness seemed spread out before me.
While I was thinking about it, the Rev. Mr.
Ingraham, who had spent seven years there,
arrived in the city. He lectured in the city at the
Marlboro' Chapel, on the results arising from
the emancipation at the British Islands. He
knew much about them, he had a station at a
mountain near Kingston, and was very desirous to have persons go there to labor. He
wished some one to go with him to his station.
He called on me with the Rev. Mr. William
Collier, to persuade me to go. I told him it was
my intention to go if I could make myself
useful, but that I was sensible that I was very
limited in education. He told me that the moral
condition of the people was very bad, and
needed labor aside from any thing else.

I left America, November 16th, 1840, in the
ship Scion, Captain Mansfield, bound for Jamaica, freighted with ice and machinery for
the silk factory. There were on board a number
of handicraftsmen and other passengers. We
sailed on Monday afternoon, from
Charlestown, Massachusetts. It rained con-

tinually until Saturday. Sunday, the 23d, was a fine day. Mr. De Grass, a young colored clergyman, was invited to perform divine service, which he did with much propriety. He spoke of the dangers we had escaped and the importance of being prepared to meet our God, (he died of fever about three weeks after arriving at Jamaica,) some who were able to attend came on deck, and listened to him with respect, while others seemed to look on in derision; these spent the afternoon and evening in card-playing. About twelve at night a storm commenced; on Monday were in great peril; the storm continued until Friday, the 27th. On that day a sail was seen at some distance making towards us, the captain judging her to be a piratical vessel, ordered the women and children below, and the men to prepare for action. The pirates were not inclined to hazard an engagement; when they saw the deck filled with armed men they left us. Thus were we preserved from the storm and from the enemy. Sabbath, 29th, divine service,—our attention was directed to the goodness of God, in sparing us.

Monday, and we mortals are still alive. Tuesday, thus far the Lord has led us on. Wednesday, thus far his power prolongs our days. Thursday, December 3d, to-day made Turks Island. Friday, this day had a view of Hayti, its lofty mountains presented a sublime prospect. Saturday, we had a glance at Cuba. Sunday,

December 6th, at six o'clock in the evening, dropped anchor at St. Ann Harbor, Jamaica. We blessed the Lord for his goodness in sparing us to see the place of our destination; and here I will mention my object in visiting Jamaica. I hoped that I might aid, in some small degree, to raise up and encourage the emancipated inhabitants, and teach the young children to read and work, to fear God, and put their trust in the Savior. Mr. Whitmarsh and his friends came on board and welcomed us. On Tuesday we went on shore to see the place and the people; my intention had been to go directly to Kingston, but the people urged me to stay with them, and I thought it my duty to comply, and wrote to Mr. Ingraham to that effect. I went first to see the minister, Mr. Abbott; I thought as he was out, I had better wait his return. The people promised to pay me for my services, or send me to Kingston. When Mr. Abbott returned he made me an offer, which I readily accepted. As I lodged in the house of one of the class-leaders I attended her class a few times, and when I learned the method, I stopped. She then commenced her authority and gave me to understand if I did not comply I should not have any pay from that society. I spoke to her of the necessity of being born of the spirit of God before we become members of the church of Christ, and told her I was sorry to see the people blinded in such a way.

She was very angry with me and soon accomplished her end by complaining of me to the minister; and I soon found I was to be dismissed, unless I would yield obedience to this class-leader. I told the minister that I did not come there to be guided by a poor foolish woman. He then told me that I had spoken something about the necessity of moral conduct in church members. I told him I had, and in my opinion, I was sorry to see it so much neglected. He replied, that he hoped I would not express myself so except to him; they have the gospel, he continued, and let them into the church. I do not approve of women societies; they destroy the world's convention; the American women have too many of them. I talked with him an hour. He paid me for the time I had been there. I continued with the same opinion, that something must be done for the elevation of the children, and it is for that I labor. I am sorry to say the meeting house is more like a play house than a place of worship. The pulpit stands about the middle of the building, behind are about six hundred children that belong to the society; there they are placed for Sabbath School, and there they remain until service is over, playing most of the time. The house is crowded with the aged and the young, the greater part of them barefooted. Some have on bonnets, but most of the women wear straw hats such as our countrymen wear.

I gave several Bibles away, not knowing that I was hurting the minister's sale, the people buy them of him at a great advance. I gave up my school at St. Ann, the 18th of March. I took the fever and was obliged to remain until the 7th of April. The people of St. Ann fulfilled their promise which they made to induce me to stop with them. On the 11th of April I arrived at Kingston, and was conducted to the Mico Institution, where Mr. Ingraham directed me to find him; he had lost his pulpit and his school, but Mr. Venning, the teacher, kindly received me. I remained there longer than I expected; the next morning he kindly sent one of the young men with me to the packet for my baggage. I then called on the American Consul, he told me he was very glad to see me for such a purpose as I had in view in visiting Jamaica, but he said it was a folly for the Americans to come to the island to better their condition; he said they came to him every day praying him to send them home.

He likewise mentioned to me the great mortality among the emigrants. The same day I saw the Rev. J. S. Beadslee, one of our missionaries, who wished me to accompany him forty miles into the interior of the country.

On May the 18th, I attended the Baptist Missionary meeting, in Queen Street Chapel; the house was crowded. Several ministers spoke of the importance of sending the gospel to Africa; they complimented the congregation on their liberality the last year, having given one hundred pounds sterling; they hoped this year they would give five hundred pounds, as there were five thousand members at the present time. There was but one colored minister on the platform. It is generally the policy of these missionaries to have the sanction of colored ministers, to all their assessments and taxes. The colored people give more readily, and are less suspicious of imposition, if one from themselves recommends the measure; this the missionaries understand very well, and know how to take advantage of it. On the 22d and 23d of June, the colored Baptists held their missionary meeting, the number of ministers, colored and mulattoes, was 18, the colored magistrates were present. The resolutions that were offered were unanimously accepted, and every thing was done in love and harmony. After taking up a contribution, they concluded with song and prayer, and returned home saying jocosely, "they would turn macroon hunters."

Mack is the name of a small coin in circulation at Jamaica. I called, on my return, at the market, and counted the different stalls. For vegetables and poultry 196, all numbered and under cover; beside 70 on the ground; these are all attended by colored women. The market is conveniently arranged, as they can close the gates and leave all safe. There are nineteen stalls for fresh fish, eighteen for pork, thirty

for beef, eighteen for turtle. These are all regular built markets, and are kept by colored
men and women. These are all in one place.
Others also may be found, as with us, all over
the city. Thus it may be hoped they are not the
stupid set of beings they have been called; here
surely we see industry; they are enterprising and
quick in their perceptions, determined to possess themselves, and to possess property besides, and quite able to take care of
themselves. They wished to know why I was
so inquisitive about them. I told them we had
heard in America that you are lazy, and that
emancipation has been of no benefit to you; I
wish to inform myself of the truth respecting
you, and give a true account on my return. Am
I right? More than two hundred people were
around me listening to what I said.

They thanked me heartily. I gave them some
tracts, and told them if it so pleased God I
would come back to them and bring them
some more books, and try what could be done
with some of the poor children to make them
better. I then left them, and went to the East
Market, where there are many of all nations.
The Jews and Spanish looked at me very black.
The colored people gathered around me. I gave
them little books and tracts, and told them I
hoped to see them again.

There are in this street upwards of a thousand young women and children, living in sin
of every kind. From thence I went to the jail,

where there were seventeen men, but no women. There were in the House of Correction three hundred culprits; they are taken from there, to work on plantations. I went to the Admiral's house, where the emigrants find a shelter until they can find employment, then they work and pay for their passage. Many leave their homes and come to Jamaica under the impression that they are to have their passage free, and on reaching the island are to be found, until they can provide for themselves.

How the mistake originated, I am not able to say, but on arriving here, strangers poor and unacclimated, find the debt for passage money hard and unexpected. It is remarkable that whether fresh from Africa, or from other islands, from the South or from New England, they all feel deceived on this point. I called on many Americans and found them poor and discontented,—rueing the day they left their country, where, notwithstanding many obstacles, their parents lived and died,—a country they helped to conquer with their toil and blood; now shall their children stray abroad and starve in foreign lands.

There is in Jamaica an institution, established in 1836, called the Mico Institution. It is named after its founder, Madame Mico, who left a large sum of money to purchase, (or rather to ransom, the one being a Christian act, the other a sin against the Holy Ghost, who expressly forbids such traffic.) Madame Mico left this money to ransom the English who were in bondage to the Algerines; if there was any left, it was to be devoted to the instruction of the colored people in the British Isles.[7]

Beside the Mico establishment, there are in Jamaica twenty-seven church missionary schools, where children are taught gratis. Whole number taught, 952. London Missionary Society Schools, sixteen; the number taught not ascertained. National Schools, thirty-eight. There are also the Wesleyan, Presbyterian and Moravian Schools; it is supposed there are private schools, where three or four thousand are educated in the city of Kingston, and twice the number in the street without the means of instruction. All the children and adults taught in the above named schools, are taxed £1 a year, except the English Church School, this is the most liberal. The Rev. Mr. Horton, a Baptist minister in Kingston, told me he had sent ninety children away from the Baptist school because they did not bring their money. It is sufficient to say they had it not to bring!

Most of the people of Jamaica are emancipated slaves, many of them are old, worn out and degraded. Those who are able to work, have yet many obstacles to contend with, and very little to encourage them; every advantage is taken of their ignorance; the same spirit of cruelty is opposed to them that held them for centuries in bondage; even religious teaching is bartered for their hard earnings, while they are allowed but thirty-three cents a day, and are told if they will not work for that they shall not work at all; an extraordinary price is asked of them for every thing they may wish to purchase, even the Bibles are sold to them at a large advance on the first purchase. Where are their apologists, if they are found wanting in the strict morals that Christians ought to practice? Who kindly says, forgive them when they err. "Forgive them, this is the bitter fruit of slavery." Who has integrity sufficient to hold the balance when these poor people are to be weighed? Yet their present state is blissful, compared with slavery.

Many of the farmers bring their produce twenty or thirty miles. Some have horses or ponys, but most of them bring their burdens on their head. As I returned from St. Andrew's Mountain, where I had been sent for by a Mr. Rose, I was overtaken by a respectable looking man on horseback; we rode about ten miles in company. The story he told me of the wrongs he and his wife had endured while in slavery, are too horrible to narrate. My heart sickens when I think of it. He asked me many questions, such as where I came from? why I came to that Isle? where had I lived, &c. I told him I was sent for by one of the missionaries to help him in his school. Indeed, said he, our color need the instruction. I asked him why the colored people did not hire for themselves? We would be very glad to, he replied, but our money is taken from us so fast we cannot. Sometimes they say we must all bring 1*l.*; to raise this, we have to sell at a loss or to borrow, so that we have nothing left for ourselves; the Macroon hunters take all—this is a nickname they give the missionaries and the class-leaders—a cutting sarcasm this!

Arrived at a tavern, about a mile from Kingston, I bade the man adieu, and stopped for my guide. The inn-keeper kindly invited me in; he asked me several questions, and I asked him as many. How do the people get along, said I, since the emancipation? The negroes, he replied, will have the island in spite of the d—. Do not you see how they live, and how much they can bear? We cannot do so. This man was an Englishman, with a large family of mulatto children. I returned with my mind fully made up what to do. Spent three weeks at the Mico establishment, and three with my colored friends from America. We thought something ought to be done for the poor girls that were destitute; they consulted with their friends, called a meeting, and formed a society of forty; each agreed to pay three dollars a year and collect, and provide a house, while I came back to America to raise the money for all needful articles for the school. Here I met Mr. Ingraham for the first time; he had come from the mountains, and his health had rapidly declined. Wishing to get his family home before the Lord took him away, he embarked for Baltimore in the Orb, and I sailed for Philadelphia, July 20th, 1841, twenty-one days from Jamaica, in good health. I found there, Fitz W. Sargent's family, from Gloucester, who I lived with when a little girl; they received me very kindly, and gave donations of books and money for that object.

I met the Anti Slavery Society at Mrs. Lucretia Motts, who took great interest in the cause.[8] I visited among the friends, and spent my time very pleasantly. August 5th, I started for New York; arrived safely, and staid with an old friend; ascertained that Mr. Ingraham's family were at Newark, at Theodore Wells'. He died four days after his arrival. I was invited to Mrs. Ingraham's, (his cousin's widow) to spend a week. There I met with much encouragement to labor in the cause. Missionaries were coming and going, and all seemed to be interested in my object. Saturday evening I went to the bath room, where I left my neck ribbon: returning after it, I had the misfortune to fall through an open trap door, down fifteen feet, on hard coal. I had no light with me. I dislocated my left shoulder, and was generally very much bruised; my screams brought the girl to my assistance, and by the help of God she brought me out of the cellar; it was some time before a surgeon could be procured; at last Dr. Josselyn came to my relief, and set my shoulder. I was obliged to remain at Mrs. Ingraham's three weeks; as soon as I was able, I left there for Boston. I intended to have gone by the western boat, but by mistake got on board Captain Comstock's, and was exposed on deck all night in a damp east wind, and when I arrived at the landing I could not assist myself; a sailor, who saw and pitied my situation, kindly took care of me and my baggage, and, on my arrival in Boston, procured a carriage for me. If it had not been for his kindness, I know not how I should have got along.

As soon as I was able, I commenced my task of collecting funds for my Free Labor School in Jamaica.[9] I collected in Boston and vicinity, in New York and Philadelphia, but not sufficient to make up the required sum, and I was obliged to take fifty dollars from my own purse, thinking that when I returned to Jamaica, they would refund the money to me. April 15th, embarked on board the brig Norma, of New York, for Jamaica. I arrived at Kingston May 6th, and found every thing different from what it was when I left; the people were in a state of agitation, several were hanged, and the insurrection was so great that it was found necessary to increase the army to quell it. Several had been hanged. On the very day I arrived a man was hanged for shooting a man as he passed through the street. Such was the state of things that it was not safe to be there.

A few young people met to celebrate their

freedom on an open plain, where they hold their market; their former masters and mistresses, envious of their happiness, conspired against them, and thought to put them down by violence. This only served to increase their numbers; but the oppressors were powerful, and succeeded in accomplishing their revenge, although many of them were relations. There was a rule among the slave holders, to take care of the children they have by their slaves; they select them out and place them in asylums. Those who lived with their white fathers were allowed great power over their slave mothers and her slave children; my heart was often grieved to see their conduct to their poor old grand parents. Those over twenty-one were freed in 1834, all under twenty-one were to serve their masters till twenty-one.[10] It is well known that at that time, the children, alike with others, received twenty-five dollars a head for their relatives. Were I to tell all my eyes have seen among that people, it would not be credited. It is well known that those that were freed, knowing their children were still in bondage, were not satisfied. In the year 1838, general freedom throughout the British Islands gave the death blow to the power of the master, and mothers received with joy their emancipated children; they no longer looked the picture of despair, fearing to see their mulatto son or daughter beating or abusing their younger brothers and sisters of a darker skin. On this occasion there was an outrage committed by those who were in power. What little the poor colored people had gathered during their four years of freedom, was destroyed by violence; their fences were broken down, and their horses and hogs taken from them. Most of the mulattoes and masters are educated, many of them are very poor, some are very rich; the property is left to the oldest daughter, she divides it with her brothers and sisters; since slavery ended many of them have married; those who are poor, and mean to live in sin, make for New Orleans and other slave States; many of the planters left the island when slavery was abolished. In June, 1841, a number of people arrived from Sierra Leone at Jamaica; these were Maroons who were banished from the island.[11] They were some of the original natives who inhabited the mountains, and were determined to destroy the whites. These Maroons would secrete themselves in trees, and arrest the whites as they passed along; they would pretend to guide them, when they would beat and abuse them as the whites did their slaves; the English, finding themselves defeated in all their plans to subdue them, proposed to take them by craft. They made a feast in a large tavern in Kingston, and invited them to come. After they had eaten, they were invited on board three ships of war that were all ready to set sail for Sierra Leone; many of them were infants in their mother's arms, they were well taken care of by the English and instructed; they were removed about the year 1796—they are bright and intelligent; I saw and conversed with them; when they heard of the abolition of slavery, they sent a petition to Queen Victoria that they might return to Jamaica, which was granted. Several of them were very old when they returned; they were men and women when they left the island, they had not forgot the injuries they had received from the hands of man, nor the mercies of God to them, nor his judgments to their enemies. Their numbers were few, but their power was great; they say the island, of right, belongs to them. Had there been a vessel in readiness, I should have come back immediately, it seemed useless to attempt to establish a Manual Labor School, as the government was so unsettled that I could not be protected. Some of my former friends were gone as teachers to Africa, and some to other parts of the island. I called on the American Consul to consult with him, he said that although such a school was much wanted, yet every thing seemed so unsettled that I had no courage to proceed. I told him there was so much excitement that I wished to leave the island as soon as he could find me a passage, it seemed useless to spend my time there. As soon as it was known that I intended to return, a movement was made to induce me to remain. I was persuaded to try the experiment for three months, not thinking their motive was bad. Before I left the United States, I got all that was needed, within fifty dollars. The fifty dollars I got from my own purse, expecting they would pay me. It cost me ten dollars for freight, and twenty-five for passage money; these people that I had hoped to serve, were much taken up with the things I had brought, they thought that I had money, and I was continually surrounded; the thought of color was no where exhibited, much notice was taken of me. I was invited to breakfast in one place, and to dine in another, &c. A society was organized, made up of men and women of authority. A constitution was drafted by my consent, by those who were appointed to meet at my rooms. Between the time of the adjournment they altered it to suit themselves. At the time appointed we came together with a spirit apparently becoming any body of Christians; most of them were members of Christian churches. The meeting was opened with reading the Scriptures and prayer. Then said the leader, since our dear sister has left her native land and her friends to come to us, we welcome her with our hearts and hands. She will dwell among us, and we will take care of her—Brethren think of it! after which he sat down, and the constitution was called for. The Preamble held out all the flattery that a fool could desire; after which they commenced the articles, supposing that they could do as they thought best. The fourth article unveiled their design. As we have designed to take care of our sister, *we the undersigned will take charge of all she has brought;* the vote was called, every person rose in a moment except myself: every eye was upon me; one asked me why I did not vote, I made no answer—they put the vote again and again, I remained seated. Well, said the President, we can do nothing without her vote; they remained some time silent, and then broke up the meeting. The next day the deacon called to see what the state of my mind was, and some of the women proposed that we should have another meeting. I told them no, I should do no more for them. As soon as they found they could not get the things in the way they intended, they started to plunder me; but I detected their design, and was on my guard. I disposed of the articles, and made ready to leave when an opportunity presented. A more skilful plan than this, Satan never designed, but the power of God was above it. It is not surprising that this people are full of deceit and lies, this is the fruits of slavery, it makes master and slaves knaves. It is the rule where slavery exists to swell the churches with numbers, and hold out such doctrines as, *obedience to tyrants,* is a duty to God. I went with a Baptist woman to the house of a minister of the Church of England, to have her grandchild christened before it died; she told me if she did not have it christened, it would rise up in judgment against her. This poor deluded creature was a class leader in the Baptist Church, and such is the condition of most of the people: they seemed blinded to every thing but money. They are great for trade, and are united in their determination for procuring property, of which they have amassed a vast amount. Notwithstanding I had made over various articles to one of the American missionaries, a Mr. J. S. O. Beadslee, of Clarendon Mountains, I also gave to others, where they were needed, which receipts and letters I have in my possession. Notwithstanding all this, they made another attempt to rob me, and as a passage could not be obtained for me to return home, I was obliged to go to the Mico establishment again for safety, such was the outrage. Houses were broken open and robbed every night. I came very near being shot: there was a certain place where we placed ourselves the first of the evening. A friend came to bring us some refreshments, I had just left the window when a gun was fired through it, by one that often sat with us; this was common in the time of slavery. Previous to vessels arriving, passages were engaged. I disposed of my articles and furniture at a very small profit. On the 1st of August, Capt. A. Miner arrived, and advertised for passengers. The American Consul procured me a passage, and on the 18th of August, myself and nine other passengers embarked for New York.

Before giving an account of the voyage from Jamaica, it may prove interesting to some readers, to have a brief description of the country. With her liberty secured to her, may she now rise in prosperity, morality, and religion, and become a happy people, whose God is the Lord.

WEST INDIES.

A denomination under which is comprehended a large chain of islands, extending in a curve from the Florida shore on the northern peninsula of America, to the Gulf of Venezuela on the southern. These islands belong to five European powers, viz: Great Britain, Spain, France, Holland, and Denmark. An inhabitant of New England can form no idea of the climate and the productions of these islands. Many of the particulars that are here mentioned, are peculiar to them all.

The climate in all the West India Islands is nearly the same, allowing for those accidental differences which the several situations and qualities of the lands themselves produce; as they lie within the tropic of Cancer, and the sun is often almost at the meridian over their heads, they are continually subjected to a heat that would be intolerable but for the trade winds, which are so refreshing as to enable the inhabitants to attend to their various occupations, even under a noonday sun; as the night advances, a breeze begins to be perceived, which blows smartly from the land, as it were from the centre towards the sea, to all points of the compass at once. The rains make the only distinction of seasons on these islands. The trees are green the year round; they have no cold or frost; our heaviest rains are but dews comparatively; with them floods of water are poured from the clouds. About May, the periodical rains from the South may be expected. Then the tropical summer, in all its splendor, makes its appearance. The nights are calm and serene, the moon shines more brightly than in New England, as do the planets and the beautiful galaxy. From the middle of August to the end of September the heat is most oppressive, the sea breeze is interrupted, and calms warn the inhabitants of the periodical rains, which fall in torrents about the first of October.

The most considerable and valuable of the British West India Islands, lies between the 75th and the 79th degrees of west longitude from London, and between 17 and 18 north latitude; it is of an oval figure, 150 miles long from east to west, and sixty miles broad in the middle, containing 4,080,000 acres. An elevated ridge, called the Blue Mountains, runs lengthwise from east to west, whence numerous rivers take their rise on both sides. The year is divided into two seasons, wet and dry. The months of July, August, and September, are called the hurricane months. The best houses are generally built low, on account of the hurricanes and earthquakes. However pleasant the sun may rise, in a moment the scene may be changed; a violent storm will suddenly arise, attended with thunder and lightning; the rain falls in torrents, and the seas and rivers rise with terrible destruction. I witnessed this awful scene in June last, at Kingston, the capital of Jamaica; the foundations of many houses were destroyed; the waters, as they rushed from the mountains, brought with them the produce of the earth, large branches of trees, together with their fruit; many perons were drowned, endeavoring to reach their homes; those who succeeded, were often obliged to travel many miles out of their usual way. Many young children, without a parent's care, were at this time destroyed. A poor old woman, speaking of these calamities to me, thus expressed herself: "Not so bad now as in the time of slavery; then God spoke very loud to *Bucker*, (the white people,) to let us go. Thank God, ever since that they give us up, we go pray, and we have it not so bad like as before." I would recommend this poor woman's remark to the fair sons and daughters of America, the land of the pilgrims. "Then God spoke very loud." May these words be engraved on the post of every door in this land of New England. God speaks very loud, and while his judgments are on the earth, may the inhabitants learn righteousness!

The mountains that intersect this island,

seem composed of rocks, thrown up by frequent earthquakes or volcanoes. These rocks, though having little soil, are adorned with a great variety of beautiful trees, growing from the fissues, which are nourished by frequent rains, and flourish in perpetual spring. From these mountains flow a vast number of small rivers of pure water, which sometimes fall in cataracts, from stupendous heights; these, with the brilliant verdure of the trees, form a most delightful landscape. Ridges of small mountains are on each side of this great chain; on these, coffee grows in great abundance; the valleys or plains between these ridges, are level beyond what is usually found in similar situations. The highest land in the island is Blue Mountain Peak, 7150 feet above the sea. The most extensive plain is thirty miles long and five broad. Black River, in the Parish of St. Elizabeth, is the only one navigable; flatboats bring down produce from plantations about thirty miles up the river. Along the coast, and on the plains, the weather is very hot; but in the mountains the air is pure and wholesome; the longest days in summer are about thirteen hours, and the shortest in winter about eleven. In the plains are found several salt fountains, and in the mountains, not far from Spanish Town, is a hot bath of great medicinal virtues; this gives relief in the complaint called the dry-bowels malady, which, excepting the bilious and yellow fevers, is one of the most terrible distempers of Jamaica. The general produce of this island is sugar, rum, molasses, ginger, cotton, indigo, pimento, cocoa, coffees, several kinds of woods, and medicinal drugs. Fruits are in great plenty, as oranges, lemons, shaddoks, citrons, pomegranates, pineapples, melons, pompions, guavas, and many others. Here are trees whose wood, when dry, is incorruptible; here is found the wild cinnamon tree, the mohogany, the cabbage, the palm, yielding an oil much esteemed for food and medicine. Here, too, is the soap tree, whose berries are useful in washing. The plantain is produced in Jamaica in abundance, and is one the most agreeable and nutritious vegetables in the world: it grows about four feet in height, and the fruit grows in clusters, which is filled with a luscious sweet pulp. The Banana is very similar to the plantain, but not so sweet. The whole island is divided into three counties, Middlesex, Surry, and Cornwall, and these into six towns, twenty parishes, and twenty-seven villages.

This island was originally part of the Spanish Empire in America, but it was taken by the English in 1656. Cromwell had fitted out a squadron under Penn and Venables, to reduce the Spanish Island of Hispaniola; but there this squadron was unsuccessful, and the commanders, of their own accord, to atone for this misfortune, made a descent on Jamaica, and having arrived at St. Jago, soon compelled the whole island to surrender.

Ever since, it has been subject to the English; and the government, next to that of Ireland, is the richest in the disposal of the crown. Port Royal was formerly the capital of Jamaica; it stood upon the point of a narrow neck of land, which, towards the sea, forms part of the border of a very fine harbor of its own name. The conveniences of this harbor, which was capable of containing a thousand sail of large ships, and of such depth as to allow them to load and unload with the greatest ease, weighed so much with the inhabitants, that they chose to build their capital on this spot, although the place was a hot, dry sand, and produced none of the necessaries of life, not even fresh water. About the beginning of the year 1692, no place for its size could be compared to this town for trade, wealth, and an entire corruption of manners. In the month of June in this year, an earthquake which shook the whole island to the foundation, totally overwhelmed this city, so as to leave, in one quarter, not even the smallest vestige remaining. In two minutes the earth opened and swallowed up nine-tenths of the houses, and two thousand people. The waters gushed out from the openings of the earth, and the people lay as it were in heaps: some of them had the good fortune to catch hold of beams and rafters of houses, and were afterwards saved by boats. Several ships were cast away in the harbor, and the Swan Frigate, which lay in the Dock, was carried over the tops of sinking houses, and did not overset, but afforded a retreat to some hundreds of people, who saved their lives upon her. An officer who was in the town at that time, says the earth opened and shut very quick in some places, and he saw several people sink down to the middle, and others appeared with their heads just above ground, and were choked to death. At Savannah above a thousand acres were sunk, with the houses and people in them, the place appearing, for some time, like a lake; this was afterwards dried up, but no houses were seen. In some parts mountains were split, and at one place a plantation was removed to the distance of a mile. The inhabitants again rebuilt the city, but it was a second time, ten years after, destroyed by a great fire. The extraordinary convenience of the harbor tempted them to build it once more, and in 1722 it was laid in ruins by a hurricane, the most terrible on record.

Such repeated calamities seemed to mark out this spot as a devoted place; the inhabitants, therefore, resolved to forsake it forever, and to reside at the opposite bay, where they built Kingston, which is now the capital of the island. In going up to Kingston, we pass over a part of and between Port Royal, leaving the mountains on the left, and a small town on the right. There are many handsome houses built there, one story high, with particos, and every convenience for those who inhabit them. Not far from Kingston stands Spanish Town, which, though at present far inferior to Kingston, was once the capital of Jamaica, and is still the seat of government.

On the 3d of October, 1780, there was a dreadful hurricane, which overwhelmed the little seaport town of Savannah, in Jamaica, and part of the adjacent country; very few houses were left standing, and a great number of lives were lost; much damage was done also, and many lives lost, in other parts of the island.

In January, 1823, a society was formed in London for mitigating and gradually abolishing slavery, throughout the British dominions, called the Anti-Slavery Society. His Royal Highness, the Duke of Gloucester, was President of the Society; in the list of Vice Presidents are the names of many of the most distinguished philanthropists of the day, and among them that of the never to be forgotton Mr. Wilberforce; as a bold champion, we see him going forward, pleading the cause of our down-trodden brethren. In the year 1834, it pleased God to break the chains from 800,000 human beings, that had been held in a state of personal slavery; and this great event was effected through the instrumentality of Clarkson, Wilberforce, and other philanthropists of the day.

The population of Jamaica is nearly 400,000; that of Kingston, the capital, 40,000. There are many places of worship of various denominations, namely, Church of England, and of Scotland, Wesleyan, the Baptist, and Roman Catholics, besides a Jewish Synagogue. These all differ from what I have seen in New England, and from those I have seen elsewhere. The Baptist hold what they call class-meetings. They have men and women deacons and deaconesses in these churches; these hold separate class–meetings; some of these can read, and some cannot. Such are the persons who hold the office of judges, and go round and urge the people to come to the class, and after they come in twice or three times, they are considered candidates for baptism. Some pay fifty cents, and some more, for being baptized; they receive a ticket as a passport into the church, paying one mark a quarter, or more, and some less, but nothing short of ten pence, that is, two English shillings a year. They must attend their class once a week, and pay three pence a week, total twelve English Shillings a year, besides the sums they pay once a month at communion, after service in the morning. On those occasions the minister retires, and the deacons examine the people, to ascertain if each one has brought a ticket; if not, they cannot commune; after this the minister returns, and performs the ceremony, then they give their money and depart. The churches are very large, holding from four to six thousand; many bring wood and other presents to their class-leader, as a token of their attachment; where there are so many communicants, these presents, and the money exacted, greatly enrich these establishments. Communicants are so ignorant of the ordinance, that they join the church merely to have a decent burial; for if they are not members, none will follow them to the grave, and no prayers will be said over them; these are borne through the streets by four men, the coffin a rough box; not so if they are church members; as soon as the news is spread that one is dying, all the class, with their leader, will assemble at the place, and join in singing hymns; this, they say, is to help the spirit up to glory; this exercise sometimes continues all night, in so loud a strain, that it is seldom that any of the people in the neighborhood are lost in sleep.

After leaving Jamaica, the vessel was tacked to a south-west course. I asked the Captain what this meant. He said he must take the current as there was no wind. Without any ceremony, I told him it was not the case, and told the passengers that he had deceived us. There were two English men that were born on the island, that had never been on the water. Before the third day passed, they asked the

Captain why they had not seen Hayti. He told them they passed when they were asleep. I told them it was not true, he was steering south south-west.[12] The passengers in the steerage got alarmed, and every one was asking the Captain what this meant. The ninth day we made land. "By——," said the Captain, "this is Key West; come, passengers, let us have a vote to run over the neck, and I will go ashore and bring aboard fruit and turtle." They all agreed but myself. He soon dropped anchor. The officers from the shore came on board and congratulated him on keeping his appointment, thus proving that my suspicions were well founded. The Captain went ashore with these men, and soon came back, called for the passengers, and asked for their vote for him to remain until the next day, saying that he could by this delay, make five or six hundred dollars, as there had been a vessel wrecked there lately. They all agreed but myself. The vessel was soon at the side of the wharf. In an hour there were twenty slaves at work to unload her; every inducement was made to persuade me to go ashore, or set my feet on the wharf. A law had just been passed there that every free colored person coming there, should be put in custody on their going ashore; there were five colored persons on board; none dared to go ashore, however uncomfortable we might be in the vessel, or however we might desire to refresh ourselves by a change of scene.[13] We remained at Key West four days.

September 3d, we set sail for New York, at 3 o'clock in the afternoon. At 10 o'clock a gale took us, that continued thirty-six hours; my state-room was filled with water, and my baggage all upset; a woman, with her little boy, and myself, were seated on a trunk thirty-six hours, with our feet pressed against a barrel to prevent falling; the water pouring over us at every breaker. Wednesday, the 9th, the sun shone out so that the Captain could take an observation. He found himself in great peril, near the coast of Texas. All hands were employed in pumping and bailing. On the eleventh, the New Orleans steamer came to our assistance; as we passed up the river, I was made to forget my own condition, as I looked with pity on the poor slaves, who were laboring and toiling, on either side, as far as could be seen with a glass. We soon reached the dock, and we were there on the old wreck a spectacle for observation; the whites went on shore and made themselves comfortable, while we poor blacks were obliged to remain on that broken, wet vessel. The people were very busy about me; one man asked me who I belonged to, and many other rude questions; he asked me where I was born; I told him Newburyport. "What were your parents' names?" I told him my father's name was Thomas Gardner; his countenance changed;

said he, "I knew him well;" and he proved friendly to me. He appeared very kind, and offered to arrange my affairs so that I might return to New York through the States. I thought it best to decline his proposal, knowing my spirit would not suffer me to pass on, and see my fellow-creatures suffering without a rebuke. We remained four days on the wreck; the boxes that contained the sugar were taken out; the two bottom tiers were washed out clean. There were a great many people that came to see the vessel; they were astonished that she did not sink; they watched me very closely. I asked them what they wished. In the mean time, there came along a drove of colored people, fettered together in pairs by the wrist; some had weights, with long chains at their ankles, men and women, young and old. I asked them what that meant. They were all ready to answer. Said they, "these negroes have been imprudent, and have stolen; some of them are free negroes from the northern ships;" "and what," I asked "are they there for?" "For being on shore, some of them at night." I asked them who made them Lord over God's inheritance. They told me I was very foolish; they should think I had suffered enough to think of myself. I looked pretty bad, it is true; I was seated on a box, but poorly dressed; the mate had taken my clothes to a washerwoman; why he took this care, he was afraid to send the cook or steward on shore, as they were colored people. I kept still; but the other woman seemed to be in perfect despair, running up and down the deck, wringing her hands and crying, at the thought of all her clothes being destroyed; then her mind dwelt upon other things, and she seemed as if she were deranged; she took their attention for a few minutes, as she was white. Soon the washer-woman came with my clothes; they spoke to her as if she had been a dog. I looked at them with as much astonishment as if I had never heard of such a thing. I asked them if they believed there was a God. "Of course we do," they replied. "Then why not obey him?" "We do." "You do not; permit me to say there is a God, and a just one, that will bring you all to account." "For what?" "For suffering these men that have just come in to be taken out of these vessels, and that awful sight I see in the streets." "O that is nothing; I should think you would be concerned about yourself." "I am sure," I replied, "the Lord will take care of me; you cannot harm me." "No; we do not wish to; we do not want you here." Every ship that comes in, the colored men are dragged to prison. I found it necessary to be stern with them; they were very rude; if I had not been so, I know not what would have been the con-sequences. They went off for that day; the next day some of them came again. "Good morn-ing," said they; "we shall watch you like the d—— until you go away; you must not say any thing to these negroes whilst you are here." "Why, then, do you talk to me, if you do not want me to say any thing to you? If you will let me alone, I will you." "Let me see your protection," they replied, "they say it is under the Russian government." I pointed them to the 18th chapter of Revelations and 15th verse: "The merchants of these things which were made rich by her, shall stand afar off, for the fear of her torment, weeping and wailing. For strong is the Lord God who judgeth her." They made no answer, but asked the Captain how soon he should get away.

On the 17th, the Captain put eight of us on board the bark H. W. Tyler, for New York; we had about a mile to walk; the Captain was in honor bound to return us our passage money, which we had paid him at Jamaica; he came without it to see if we were there, and went away saying he would soon return with it; but we saw no more of him or our money! Our bark, and a vessel loaded with slaves, were towed down the river by the same steamer; we dropped anchor at the bottom of the bay, as a storm was rising. The 18th, on Sabbath, it rained all day. Capt. Tyler knocked at my door, wishing me to come out; it rained hard; the bulwark of the bark was so high I could not look over it; he placed something for me to stand on, that I might see the awful sight, which was the vessel of slaves laying at the side of our ship! the deck was full of young men, girls, and children, bound to Texas for sale! Monday, the 19th, Capt. Tyler demanded of us to pay him for our passage. I had but ten dollars, and was determined not to give it; he was very severe with all. I told him there were articles enough to pay him belonging to me. Those who had nothing, were obliged to go back in the steamer. Tuesday, the 20th, we set sail; the storm was not over. The 22d the gale took us; we were dismasted, and to save sinking, sixty casks of molasses were stove in, and holes cut in the bulwarks to let it off. All the fowls, pigs, and fresh provisions were lost. We were carried seventy-five miles up the bay of Mexico. The Captain was determined not to pay the steamer for carrying him back to New Orleans, and made his way the best he could.

The 3d of October we arrived again at Key West. The Captain got the bark repaired, and took on board a number of turtles, and a plenty of brandy. Friday, the 7th, set sail for New York; the Captain asked me why I did not go ashore when there in the Comet; "had you," said he, "they intended to beat you. John and Lucy Davenport, of Salem, laid down the first ten dollars toward a hundred for that person who should get you there." The Florida laws are about the same as those at New Orleans. He was very talkative: wished to know if I saw anything of the Creole's crew while at Jamaica. I told him they were all safe, a fine set of young men and women; one dear little girl, that was taken from her mother in Virginia, I should have taken with me, if I had had the money. He said his brother owned the Creole, and some of the slaves were his. "I never owned any; I have followed the sea all my life, and can tell every port and town in your State."

October 19th, 1842, arrived at New York, and thankful was I to set my feet on land, almost famished for the want of food; we lost all of our provisions; nothing was left but sailors' beef, and that was tainted before it was salted. I went at once to those who professed to be friends, but found myself mistaken. I hardly knew what was best. I had put up at Mrs. Rawes'; she did all she could to raise the twenty-five dollars that I must pay before I could take my baggage from the vessel. This seemed hard to obtain; I travelled from one to another for three days; at last I called at the Second Advent office; Mr. Nath'l Southard left his business at once, and took me to Mr. Lewis Tappan, and others; he raised the money, and went with me to the ship after my baggage.[14] It was three o'clock on Saturday afternoon when I called on Mr. Southard; the vessel and Captain belonged to Virginia, was all ready for sea, waiting for a wind; they had ransacked my things. I took from Jamaica forty dollars' worth of preserved fruits; part were lost when we were cast away in the Comet, and some they had stolen. At 8 o'clock on Saturday evening, I made out to have my things landed on the wharf; it was very dark, as it rained hard. My kind friend did not leave me until they were all safely lodged at my residence. I boarded there three weeks, thinking to come home; but it was thought best for me to wait, and see if Capt. Miner came or not, hoping that I might recover my loss through him. I took a room, and went to sewing, and found the people very kind.

February, 1843, the colored men that went back to New Orleans, for the want of passage money, arrived at New York, wearied out. All the white people remained there. I waited in New York until the last of July, when I started for Boston. August 1st, 1843, arrived, poor in health, and poor in purse, having sacrificed both, hoping to benefit my fellow creatures. I trust it was acceptable to God, who in his providence preserved me in perils by land, and perils by sea.

> "God moves in a mysterious way
>   His wonders to perform;
> He plants his footsteps on the sea,
>   And rides upon the storm.
>
> "Deep in unfathomable mines
>   Of never failing skill,
> He treasures up his bright designs,
>   And works his sovereign will."

Having lost all, I determined, by the help of God, to leave the event; some of my friends in this city sympathized with me, and others took the advantage to reproach me. But in the hands of the Lord there is a cup; the Saviour drank it to the dregs. They gather themselves together; they hide themselves; they mark my steps; they waited for my soul, but the Lord is my defence, the Holy one of Israel is my Saviour. I'll trust him for strength and defence. What things were gain to me, I counted loss for Christ, for whom I have suffered all things; and do count them nothing, that I may win Christ, and be found in him, not having mine own righteousness, which is of the law, but that which is through the faith of Christ, that which is of God by faith, that I may know him, and the power of his resurrection, and the fellowship of his sufferings, being made conformable unto his death, strengthened with all might, according to his glorious power, unto all patience and long-suffering, with joyfulness, thinking it not strange concerning the fiery trials, as though some strange thing happened; for saith the apostle, it is better if the will of God so be that ye suffer for well doing, than for evil; they think it strange that ye run not with them to the same excess of riot, speaking evil of you. If they do these things in a green tree, what shall be done in a dry!

"I hate to walk, I hate to sit
   With men of vanity and lies;
The scoffer and the hypocrite
   Are the abhorrence of my eyes.

God knows their impious thoughts are vain,
   And they shall feel his power;

His wrath shall pierce their souls with pain,
  In some surprising hour."

The first twenty months after my arrival in the city, notwithstanding my often infirmities, I labored with much success, until I hired with and from those with whom I mostly sympathized, and shared in common the disadvantages and stigma that is heaped upon us, in this our professed Christian land. But my lot was like the man that went down from Jerusalem, and fell among thieves, which stripped him of his raiment, and wounding him, departed, leaving him half dead. What I did not lose, when cast away, has been taken from my room where I hired. Three times I had been broken up in business, embarrassed and obliged to move, when not able to wait on myself. This has been my lot. In the midst of my afflictions, sometimes I have thought my case like that of Paul's, when cast among wild beats. "Had not the Lord been on my side, they would have swallowed me up; but blessed be the Lord who hath not given me a prey to their teeth."

In 1848 and '49 the Lord was pleased to lay his hand upon me. Some of my friends came to my relief; but the promises of God were neither few nor small; he knows them that trust and fear him. No one has greater reason to be grateful than I. God has preserved me through much suffering the past winter. I have passed through another furnace of affliction, and may

God's dispensations be sanctified to me. The sufferings of this present life are not worthy to be compared with the glory that shall be revealed hereafter. Who shall separate us from the love of Christ? Shall tribulation, or distress, or persecution, or famine, or nakedness, or peril, or sword? Nay, in all these things we are more than conquerors, through him that loved us, and gave himself for us. Soon he will come; here we live by faith; if any one draw back, my soul shall have no pleasure in him.

Truly the promises of God are given for our encouragement; they are yea and amen, in Christ Jesus; they are a covert from the storm, a shelter from the heat, a sure retreat for the weary and way worn traveller.

Many are the trials and temptations to which we are exposed in this vale of tears, but in heaven we shall be free from the bondage of sin. Nothing can enter there to annoy or molest the redeemed ones: the Captain of our salvation was made perfect through suffering; he was despised and rejected of men, a man of sorrows, and acquainted with grief; and that he might sanctify the people with his own blood, suffered without the gate. Let us go forth, therefore, unto him, bearing his reproach. Here we have no continuing city nor abiding place.

I have much to be thankful to God for; for the comforts of this life, and the kind friends who have so kindly bestowed their favors upon me, and while they in this life have an abundance, may they have the presence of God; and when the King shall come, may they have their lamps trimmed and burning: then shall he say, "Come ye blessed of my Father, inherit the kingdom prepared for you from the foundation of the world: for I was an hungered, and ye gave me meat, I was thirsty, and ye gave me drink, naked, and ye clothed me, sick, and in prison, and ye visited me. Then shall the righteous answer, saying: when saw we thee an hungered, and fed thee, and thirsty, and gave thee drink, naked, and clothed thee, sick, and in prison, and ministered unto thee, or a stranger, and took thee in?" And the King shall answer and say: "Inasmuch as ye have done it unto one of the least of my disciples, ye have done it unto me. The poorest can do something for the cause of Christ; even a cup of cold water, given with a desire to benefit a fellow creature, will be acceptable to God. May the power of God, and the spirit of Christ rule and reign in all hearts. He knoweth them that love and trust in him."

I am a wonder unto many, but the Lord is my strong refuge, and in him will I trust. I shall fear no evil, for thou, O Lord, art ever near to shield and protect thy dependent children. Underneath him is the everlasting arm of mercy; misfortune is never mournful for the soul that accepts it, for such do always see that every cloud is an angel's face; sorrow connects the soul with the invisible.

O Father, fearful indeed is this world's pilgrimage, when the soul has learned that all its sounds are echoes, all its sights are shadows. But lo! a cloud opens, a face serene and hopeful looks forth and saith, "Be thou as a little child, and thus shalt thou become a seraph, and bow thyself in silent humility and pray, not that afflictions might not visit, but be willing to be purified through fire, and accept it meekly."

THE HIDING PLACE.

Amid this world's tumultuous noise,
For peace my soul to Jesus flies;
If I've an interest in his grace,
I want no other hiding place.

The world with all its charms is vain,
Its wealth and honors I disdain:
All its extensive aims embrace,
Can ne'er afford a hiding place.

A guilty, sinful heart is mine,
Jesus, unbounded love is thine!
When I behold thy smiling face,
'Tis then I see my hiding place.

To save, if once my Lord engage,
The world may laugh, and Satan rage:
The powers of hell can ne'er erase
My name from God's own hiding place.

I'm in a wilderness below,
Lord, guide me all my journey through,
Plainly let me thy footsteps trace,
Which lead to heaven, my hiding place.

Should dangers thick impede my course,
O let my soul sustain no loss;
Help me to run the Christian race,
And enter safe my hiding place.

Then with enlarged powers,
I'll triumph in redeeming love,
Eternal ages will I praise
My Lord for such a hiding place.

ENDNOTES:
THE NARRATIVE OF MRS. PRINCE

[1] Winthrop Sargent was a native of Gloucester, Massachusetts, and a man of varied intellectual interests. Although Mrs. Prince calls him "Captain," he rose to the rank of major in the Continental Army and later became the first territorial governor of Mississippi.

[2] The "Parsons family" produced two noted jurists, both named Theophilus. The family moved from Newburyport in 1800, shortly after Nancy Prince's birth and her father's death.

[3] Here, and later in the paragraph, Mrs. Prince probably means "step-father" rather than "father-in-law."

[4] Cholera's devastation was fresh in the minds of Mrs. Prince's readers. It first struck in the United States in 1832, a year after its occurrence in Russia. It appeared again in 1849, just prior to publication of the *Narrative,* and was fatal to about half the people who contracted the disease. The fact that cholera thrived in unsanitary conditions and in poorer, vice-ridden neighborhoods helped reinforce the view expressed by Mrs. Prince that it was God's judgment on human sinfulness.

[5] Mrs. Prince is referring to serfs, whose situation was not precisely equivalent to that of American slaves in that they were generally of the same race as their masters and often received a small plot of land to cultivate for themselves, in addition to the land they cultivated for the master (Kolchin, pp. 43–46).

[6] This is not the same Mrs. Mott whom Mrs. Prince mentions later. The "physician" referred to here is Mrs. Elizabeth Mott, who, in Boston with her husband, dispensed "Systematic Vegetable Medicine"—a form of medication frowned upon by "regular" physicians but much favored by reformers. She was also the author of a book of medical advice for women.

[7]Lady Mico left her bequest of £1,000 in 1670. Thanks to the decline of piracy and the resulting shortage of Christians to redeem from their captivity, the sum had risen to £120,000 by 1828, when an abolitionist member of Parliament suggested it be used for "the promotion of education in the British Colonies."

[8]Lucretia Mott, and her husband James, were famous Quaker abolitionists, They—Lucretia especially—were also involved in early feminist activities; both participated in the Woman's Rights Convention in 1854 at which Mrs. Prince spoke.

[9]Free Labor Schools, or "Manual Labor Schools," as Mrs. Prince also calls them, were a popular idea in her day, particularly among religiously-minded reformers. Students provided a certain amount of labor in return for their education.

[10]At points in this paragraph, Mrs. Prince's language is confusing, and, on some issues, mistaken. She is not referring to all Afro-Jamaican children, but rather to some who fell under a provision of the Emancipation Act. Although it freed children under six years of age in 1834, the law made it possible for mothers to apprentice them to masters until they reached twenty-one. It was such children she had in mind when she wrote this passage; she uses "serve" and "bondage" to refer to apprenticeship, rather than slavery. For the details of the Act's provisions, see the Introduction.

[11]Maroons were freed or runaways slaves who fled to the interior of Jamaica and maintained an independent (and troublesome) presence in defiance of white authority.

[12]Mrs. Prince may not have been right about all the details regarding the ship's course. Her experience with seafaring may nonetheless have alerted her to the captain's deception.

[13]Mrs. Prince is referring to a type of law, first passed in South Carolina in 1822 and widely copied by other Southern states, which permitted the imprisonment of free African-American sailors while their ships were in port. The intention was to prevent them from spreading dangerous ideas about freedom to local blacks.

[14]Lewis Tappan and his brother Arthur were wealthy and pious New York merchants who donated much money and organizational ability to a variety of causes, including the anti-slavery movement and assorted Christian projects.